Endorse:

"*Lessons from a School Shooti* inspirational, but it is filled wit̲ ̲ ̲ ̲ ̲ ̲ ̲ ̲ ̲ ̲ ̲ ̲ ̲ for life that our youth need for the challenges of today. As an educator, I would use Missy's story and the lessons that follow each chapter to engage teens in honest discussions and relevant activities to fuel the heart and ignite the mind."

–Tim Hanner, *2010 Kentucky Superintendent of the Year, founder of NaviGo College and Career Prep Services*

"This book touched me in ways that are impossible to describe. As both a school shooting survivor and a high school teacher, I highly recommend it for anyone in education— from administrators to curriculum designers to classroom teachers. We can all learn from Missy's words how to spread a little more love and empathy."

–Heather Martin, *Columbine High School shooting survivor, teacher, and co-founder of The Rebels Project*

"Once again, Missy Jenkins Smith addresses a highly relevant but difficult topic in a meaningful and impactful way. This book, inspired by Missy's passion for students, will help teachers, administrators, and education professionals as they deal with escalating episodes of violence in America's schools."

–C. Ed Massey, *past president of the National School Boards Association, board member for Boone County (Ky.) Schools*

"This book is not about being a victim of a school shooting, but about how to live a life of strength, optimism, and kindness. It is not a story of difficulties and struggles, but about trying to improve the world one person at a time. This is a book for everyone who wants to make a real positive difference in the lives of others."

–Bill Bond, *safe schools specialist for the National Association of Secondary School Principals, former principal at Heath High School in Paducah, Kentucky*

"This uplifting book shows how Missy has dealt with adversity and how she has managed to stay on a positive track in life, especially through her interactions with both negative and positive people. School-aged kids, along with adults, could definitely learn what it truly means to 'Be Kind' to others while using six simple principles in their everyday lives. I cannot wait to share this book and promote it in schools."

"Missy does a beautiful job communicating the profound, foundational importance of exercising six seemingly simple principles in our everyday life: listening, empathy, forgiveness, laughter, optimism, and kindness. We come to learn that while these six principles might appear simple in theory, it takes true dedication and open-mindedness to embody them in practice. With Missy's guidance and example, you learn throughout the book how you might meaningfully apply these same principles in your own life. Missy's refreshing perspective and optimism will inspire you and remind you in the capacity of others to do and be good."

—Ashley Cech, *gun violence prevention activist and daughter of Yvonne Cech, a librarian who survived the Sandy Hook Elementary School shooting*

Lessons from a School Shooting Survivor
How to Find the Good in Others and
Live a Life of Love and Peace

Missy Jenkins Smith
with William Croyle

Lessons from a School Shooting Survivor
How to Find the Good in Others and Live a Life of Love
and Peace
by Missy Jenkins Smith with William Croyle

Cover layout: Author Packages
Back Cover photograph: Tate Graham

ISBN: 978-0-9995238-0-3

Dedication

To the students I have worked with in day treatment, and to all the youth around the world. May this book help you find the love, peace, and hope you so desire and deserve.

Contents

Note: The Take Action! section at the end of each chapter has been designed with school classrooms in mind, though all of the activities can be done at home or in other settings, such as at work or in social groups. While some of the activities may be better suited for specific audiences, such as an elementary school class rather than a middle or high school class, most of them can be effectively performed by people of all ages, including adults.

Introduction

EVERYONE HAS A STORY, one that is different from yours and mine.

Think about somebody you cross paths with but with whom you don't interact much. It could be a classmate, a teammate, a teacher, a neighbor, or someone on the bus. What is her story? I mean her *real* story. The one stuffed deep inside her soul that would explain her personality, behavior, or attitude. The one that would reveal why she does what she does, thinks the way she thinks, loves what she loves, or hates what she hates. The one that would divulge the reasons behind her seemingly odd quirks or habits. The story that could give you a completely different perspective of her—a kinder one—if you only knew it.

No two people are born alike or raised the same. That's no secret. Yet, inexplicably and far too often, we make unnecessary judgments and assumptions about one another. We view others according to the music they listen to, the grades they get in school, the kids they hang out with, the way they talk, the clothes they wear, the cell phone they use, the political candidates they support, their religion, their non-religion, their nationality, or their skin color. We choose to see them in light of our own values, statuses, or backgrounds instead of accepting them for who they are and embracing our differences. This attitude is especially prevalent on social media sites, where we callously judge people based on a single comment or photo or video without learning their story—or at least respecting that they have one.

Our world today is at a crossroads. The hatred, violence, and lack of compassion toward each other, reflected in our words and actions and usually without good reason, are clearly evident. Yet, to the contrary, people also frequently post on social media and tell me firsthand that they are tired of the incessant negativity and are desperately longing for unfailing love and peace in their lives. How can we expect to receive such splendor if we aren't willing to consistently offer it to one another? I wonder how many of us have become so entrenched in our negative dialogue and habits that we aren't even cognizant of our boorish behavior and its detrimental effects on ourselves and those around us.

Through my hundreds of talks over the past two decades, and in my work for more than ten years as a day treatment counselor for troubled teenagers, I have come to realize that love and peace can often be achieved through two practices: *always* respecting that everyone has a unique story, and applying to *every* aspect of our daily lives the six principles of listening, empathy, forgiveness, laughter, optimism, and kindness.

They're simple words, but each one comes with a heavy responsibility. We just can't say, "I forgave my friend this morning, and I did something kind for a classmate this afternoon, so I can cross those off my list." That attitude would be applying your life to the principles, which won't substantially change anything, rather than applying the principles to your life, which can change *everything*.

We must take every single moment from the time we awake until we go to sleep—each situation we're in, each word we speak, each reaction we have, each task we do, each thought we form, each gesture we show—and apply these principles until they become habit. All day and every day we must set the intention to listen, to empathize, to forgive...

Sound exhausting? I didn't say this would be easy. It's a lot to swallow. For some people, especially the cynical ones, this will require a life-changing shift in the way they view others and process information. It will require them to start a brand new chapter in their own story. But there's an old saying that nothing worthwhile is easy, and I can't think of anything more worthwhile than everyone being nice to each other.

Understand that taking this course of action does not mean we aren't allowed to get upset, frustrated, annoyed, or angry at someone or at a certain situation. It does not mean we shouldn't defend ourselves when necessary. It does not even mean we have to like everybody. We're human, far from perfect. But, as Anne Frank said, "In spite of everything I still believe that people are really good at heart."

We are all born with a basic goodness. I know—we look at the way some people behave and say, "No way was he ever a good person!" But even people we would classify as the world's worst were born sweet, innocent, and without prejudice. It was primarily the influences in their lives that made them, or at least put them on the path toward, who they are today. That basic goodness, however, is still within them. Our collective goal should be to harness it out of as many people as possible and as often as possible, beginning with ourselves.

If you don't know my story, I was shot when I was fifteen years old. The bullet entered the front of me and exited the back of me. Can you imagine? Not only that, but it happened in school, and at a time when school shootings were an anomaly. I watched three classmates die right in front of me on the floor of the lobby. I'm in a wheelchair today and likely for the rest of my life because the bullet from the boy who shot me, who was just fourteen years old then, pierced my spine and paralyzed me from the chest down.

The shooting instantly altered my perspective of just about everything. The first time I put on my shirt and pants by myself as a paraplegic took me forty-five exasperating minutes. A simple street curb had become like a rugged mountain as I struggled to maneuver my wheelchair over it. The teachers who selflessly raced to our aid during the gunfire weren't just educators who taught us math or English; they were heroes who risked their lives to save us. I learned to appreciate more of the little joys in life, from the sunrise in the morning to the stars at night and all the people I encountered in between.

I realized that violence is not the answer, but that if it is love and peace we so desire, we can't expect them to magically occur; we have to work for them. We have to strive to be on the same page with one another. That's tricky considering there are more than seven billion people with more than seven billion different stories on this vast planet. But I really do believe that if we all respect each other's stories and apply the principles to everything we do each day, it is absolutely possible to revolutionize the world.

One of my favorite hymns is "Let There Be Peace on Earth." While most often heard in churches, the song is universal, applying to those who believe in a higher power as well as to a secular audience. The second verse is gripping: "Let peace begin with me, let this be the moment now. With every step I take, let this be my solemn vow: to take each moment and live each moment in peace eternally. Let there be peace on earth, and let it begin with me."

It begins with you, and it begins with me. A transformation as massive as the one I am about to present requires that we work together with unbridled ambition. If you still aren't too sure about this, I just ask that you give it a chance. Give *me* a chance. You have nothing to lose, and the potential reward is immense.

Let's do this together…starting right now.

My Story

"I believe that I speak for every American in sending our thoughts and prayers to the parents of Kayce Steger, Jessica James, Nicole Hadley, and the wounded children and the entire community of West Paducah."
–President Bill Clinton, December 2, 1997

I F YOU'VE READ MY memoir, *I Choose to be Happy: A School Shooting Survivor's Triumph over Tragedy*, you know the good, the bad, and the ugly of my life—and thank you for reading it! It has certainly been a fascinating journey thus far, to say the least. For those who have not read it, and to refresh the memories of those who have, here are some of the highlights and lowlights of my story since the day of the shooting.

My twin sister, Mandy, and I rode to Heath High School with our friends, Taylor and Carrie, the morning of December 1, 1997. It was the Monday after our four-day Thanksgiving break. We entered the building just in time for the start of the 7:35 A.M. prayer circle, a daily gathering of a few dozen students in the lobby. Though Heath was a public school, Paducah is on the upper edge of the nation's Bible Belt with many people of faith, so to have such a custom was not out of the ordinary or controversial to anyone. We all respected each other's beliefs and non-beliefs. I had been baptized in my church just two years earlier, so the circle was certainly something I looked forward to each day. We would all hold hands and make prayer requests. The student leader would then say a final prayer before we would disperse for class. It lasted a few minutes and was an invigorating way for me to start each day.

There was nothing unusual happening that morning, at least from my standpoint. I woke up a little late, but I got dressed quickly and out of the house in time to catch our ride. Our ten- to fifteen-minute drive to school was uneventful. I was a sophomore and had a test to take during first period in World Civ, but I was ready for it—at least as ready as a teenager coming off a long holiday weekend could be. The prayer circle had the typical people in it. Those who weren't in it hung out in the lobby outside the circle and talked about their weekend, or they crammed in some last-second studying before the first bell.

After the final prayer, I walked to my right toward a nearby pillar where I had left my book bag. Mandy was walking behind me. Just before I reached down for the bag, I heard a loud pop. I looked to my left, toward the center of the lobby, and saw freshman Nicole Hadley drop to the ground. I then heard two more pops about a second apart, and then several more in rapid succession. I assumed someone was shooting fireworks as a prank and Nicole was in on it.

It was during those final shots that my body went numb, and I fell to the floor. I was on my back staring straight at the ceiling with no idea why. I felt no immediate pain, but I couldn't move. Students screamed and stampeded past me, out of the lobby and down the long hallway toward the gym, in the opposite direction of where Nicole lay. Mandy had fallen at about the same time I had after she felt something scrape the back of her neck and breeze through her hair. She didn't know at the time that it had been a bullet. When she saw me on the floor, she instinctively crawled over and threw herself on top of me. I still didn't know I'd been shot or why I couldn't move. I asked Mandy multiple times what was happening.

"There's a gun," she finally said, her voice trembling.

A gun? What? "Who's got a gun?" I asked.

"Michael Carneal," she replied.

Michael was a freshman, a year younger than us, but someone we considered a friend. We were in band together and had known each other for years. He was generally a quiet kid, but he was also very funny with a great sense of humor. We'd never had any issues with him. It was illogical to me that anyone in our school would have a gun, especially him.

The next several minutes were complete chaos. My friend and classmate, Kayce Steger, had been shot and was laying face down just a few feet away from me on the other side of the pillar. Jessica James, a senior, had been standing at my feet trying to help those of us who had been wounded when she suddenly went into convulsions; she too had been shot, but it took several seconds before she felt the effects. Four other students also had been hit. Nicole, Kayce, and Jessica would all die from their wounds. I faded in and out of consciousness as two of my teachers knelt next to me and prayed while trying to keep me awake and prevent me from moving. Several minutes later, after I was finally loaded onto a gurney and into an ambulance with Kayce, I hopelessly

3

watched medical personnel try to revive her on our ride to the hospital.

This was my Monday morning. In school. I would never take that World Civ exam. I was just fifteen years old.

*****

Paducah is a small, tight-knit community of about twenty-five thousand citizens in western Kentucky, across the Ohio River from Illinois. If you ask people outside of Paducah who were old enough to remember the shooting when it happened if they still remember it today, many will say no, even though it likely had a significant impact on them when it occurred. The reason they don't recall it now is that it was just the second school shooting in a string of dozens of them the past two decades (the first was in Pearl, Mississippi, exactly two months earlier). Quite sadly, because there have been so many, they have blended together, causing the tragedy at Heath to fade from memory. Today, some school shootings don't even make headlines.

The Heath shooting happened three months before Jonesboro, sixteen months before Columbine, more than nine years before Virginia Tech, and fifteen years before Sandy Hook. It caused the entire world to pause because school shootings were so rare. Worldwide media flocked to Paducah and set up camp. We were the lead story on every major news channel and in nearly every newspaper across the country and around the world—for days. There was one funeral for Nicole, Kayce, and Jessica, and it was aired live on CNN. I received hundreds upon hundreds of letters and packages every day for weeks from people in countries I'd never heard of and in languages I couldn't read, and that was before the Internet when locating people wasn't easy. Some of the letters arrived simply with the address of "Missy Jenkins, Paducah, Kentucky."

The shooting was *that* big of a deal.

The hospital staff took X-rays of me, performed some tests, and even found the bullet. It had gone into the left side of my chest just above my heart, hit my spine, and exited the right side of my back. My spine must have slowed its momentum; they found the bullet lodged between my back and my shirt.

Doctors determined that surgery would not help and might even make my condition worse. They said I was paralyzed from the chest down and would probably never walk again. I think I figured as much before they told me, and I accepted my fate better than one might expect. I didn't cry or complain. Maybe it was due to my faith. Maybe I was in shock. Maybe it was the effects of the pain medication they had administered. Probably a little of all three. Whatever the reason, I immediately understood and accepted that this was going to be my new life.

I would find out the next day about the deaths of the three girls. I don't recall my reaction because I was hooked to a bunch of tubes, heavily drugged on morphine, and unable to sit up. I would somberly watch their funeral a few days later on television from the intensive care unit. I would spend several months in a hospital and in rehab facilities, trying to learn to live again. Everything I had once taken for granted—walking, getting dressed, reaching high shelves, getting in and out of bed or a car, passing through doorways, and even going to the bathroom like everyone else—was at best extremely difficult, and at worst impossible.

I became a fixation with the media when my doctors and family publicly stated that I was paralyzed, but that I was in good spirits and ready for my new challenges. I guess my attitude made me a beacon of hope, something everyone needed and wanted to hold on to during such a horrific time. One day, when I was being transferred on a gurney from one hospital building to another, members of the media literally chased after me. I laughed when I first noticed security guards escorting me. Was that really necessary? Turns out it was. You'd have thought I was some Hollywood A-list celebrity the way reporters were tripping over each other, shoving microphones in my face, and shouting questions at me.

I had been a pretty introverted person most of my life, but I eventually let the *Paducah Sun* newspaper and national television show *Dateline* into my hospital room one day to satisfy the curiosity seekers. That's when I realized how therapeutic it was to speak publicly about what had happened, so I did more of it. A *lot* more.

I would give interviews in the weeks, months, and years ahead to pretty much any local and national media that wanted to speak to me, including *Good Morning America, Oprah, Inside Edition, Today, Montel Williams,* and *Anderson Cooper 360. People* magazine even showed up to a school dance to write an article, and *Ladies' Home Journal* named me one of its "Most Fascinating Women," an honor that I still can't believe today. I was the only non-celebrity on the list that included women like actresses Whoopi Goldberg, Queen Latifah, and Drew Barrymore.

I returned to school at the end of my sophomore year. It was never a question of if I would return, but when. A lot of people expected me to transfer schools or be home schooled, but those ideas had never crossed my mind. Heath was my home. That's where my friends were. It's where I wanted to be and where I belonged.

My first day back, I wheeled myself into the lobby and asked Mandy to re-enact what had happened during the shooting. It was the elephant in the room that I wanted to face head on to help me continue moving forward with my life. No way was I going to let Michael's actions affect me more than they already had.

My rehab was extensive during high school. I missed a lot of instruction, but I kept up my grades and graduated with my class in 2000. I even stood from my wheelchair to receive my diploma with the help of a brace developed by Los Angeles physician Dr. Roy Douglas, a brace I would use several years later to dance with my husband at our wedding and still use occasionally today. I also did some fun and exciting things just prior to and after graduation, such as compete in the Los Angeles Marathon, meet the Backstreet Boys, participate in a roundtable discussion on youth violence at the White House with President Bill Clinton, compete in and win the Miss Wheelchair Kentucky pageant, take part in an MTV special on school bullying, and speak at the Democratic National Convention as Vice President Al Gore's guest. The adage "When one door closes, another opens" certainly applied to me. Some doors had been slammed shut because of my paralysis, but plenty of new ones had opened wide.

I attended college at Murray State University in southwest Kentucky, about forty-five minutes from my Paducah home. I graduated with a degree in social work, joined the Alpha Omicron Pi sorority, and met my future husband there. Josh Smith and I hit it off immediately when we met at a fraternity party. Well, almost immediately. When I called him after the party, he was asleep when he answered the phone. No joke. He answered the phone and was snoring into it. And then, a couple days later, on our first date at my house, he fell asleep during the movie we were watching. I couldn't help but wonder, *Am I really that boring?*

Fortunately, he would wake up in time to marry me in the summer of 2006, and we would remain in Murray where we still live today. Josh and I have two wild but wonderful boys, Logan and Carter, along with several chickens and other animals on our sixty-acre farm. Josh works as a physical education teacher and football coach in one of our local school districts, and I work in the same district as a day treatment counselor for troubled teenagers. I worked there for ten years before taking a couple years off to speak full time, but I have since returned and have arranged with my boss to also be able to continue speaking.

The day treatment center serves as both a behavioral treatment center and a school. Students who struggle to function in a mainstream classroom come to day treatment and stay until they develop the skills necessary to return to their regular classroom. I wanted to work in day treatment as soon as I graduated from college. My hope was to use my experience in the shooting to help students overcome their problems, and I found after being away from it for the two years I spoke full time that I really missed it. It is not easy work by any means, but when I am able to help a kid turn his or her life around and negate the potential to hurt others like Michael did, it is as rewarding as any job could be.

*****

The three primary questions most people ask me about Michael are: "What happened to him after the shooting?" "Where did he get the guns?" and "Why did he do what he did?" Michael never went on trial because he admitted to what he did. About a year after the shooting, he was sentenced to life in prison without the chance of parole for twenty-five years. He spent some time in a juvenile facility, and then he was moved to a state prison near Louisville, Kentucky, once he was old enough, where he remains today.

During his early years behind bars he wrote me letters and even called my house a couple times. Yes, it freaked me out. I never responded to the letters, and my dad spoke with authorities to make sure the calls stopped. I finally did meet with him face to face in the summer of 2007, about a month before my son Logan was born. The meeting was my idea, and one Michael was open to. I thought talking to him could bring some semblance of closure for me and help me with my talks to students. I was more scared than I had expected I would be, especially when we pulled up to the prison gates, but there was no turning back. Mandy and I were escorted into a room just inside the prison, sat across from Michael at a table, and we spent two hours calmly conversing about the shooting and our lives since. It was a surreal two hours, but one that I believe benefitted both of us. Details of that meeting are in my memoir, and I will share a little bit more about it later in this book.

Michael stole the guns and ammunition from his friend's house. The friend's dad had guns and ammo locked in his garage, but Michael knew where he kept the key. Michael climbed through an unlocked garage window, took what he wanted, and was able to ride away on his bike with everything in tow. The morning of the shooting, he put a gun and the ammo in his backpack, and he also wrapped some guns inside a blanket. When his sister asked him what was in the blanket as he set it in her trunk before they left for school, he casually told her it was supplies for a school project. She had no reason not to believe him. When he got to the lobby, while the prayer circle was in session, he stood in the corner loading the .22-caliber semi-automatic pistol he had pulled from his backpack. Nobody noticed. He then randomly fired the gun several times before setting it down on the floor of his own volition. Our principal, Bill Bond, grabbed Michael's arm and hustled him into a nearby office.

There is no excuse whatsoever for Michael's actions, but I'm not sure there is one clear-cut answer as to why he did what he did. Some believe he was aiming for those of us in the prayer circle because he wanted to kill Christians in the school. I have never believed that, and there is no evidence I'm aware of that that was ever the case. In fact, Michael was a Christian himself who had been confirmed in his church earlier that year.

His rampage has also been blamed on schizophrenia, a diagnosis he received from psychologists who had evaluated him in prison. That I do believe to an extent. He had claimed during those evaluations that he had heard voices in his head many times leading up to the shooting, and it was obvious by the content of the many letters he wrote to me over the years that something just wasn't right about him.

The shooting has also been blamed on bullying. Some say he was bullied so much for so long that he decided to finally take matters into his own hands. I know there is definitely truth to that, and he told me some of the stories when we met in prison. The bullying Michael had endured from other students was extensive, far more than I or most people were ever aware. He was frequently called names and spit on. He was hazed by other band members. He once had a science project destroyed by a student just before class, and he sometimes had his lunch stolen in the cafeteria. He told me that one time someone punched him so hard in the kidneys that he urinated blood. And when he was in middle school, an article in the school newspaper implied that he was gay. How that made it past editors, I have no idea, but it happened. That's just some of the bullying he faced, and a topic I will discuss more as I address the six principles.

Life has generally been good for me since my meeting with him, but I have suffered a lot of loss during that time. In a six-year period, beginning in 2009, I lost my cousin and best friend, Brad Brewer, who died of cancer at the age of thirty-six; my oldest sister, Pam, who died of a stroke at the age of forty-five; my mom, a saint of a woman, at the age of sixty-nine; my nephew, Winston, who was a student at Heath with me the day of the shooting and a very close friend; and my dad, my hero, who died of health complications at the age of seventy-six.

Losing all of those people hurt deeply, but nothing ripped out my heart more than losing both of my parents when I was still in my early thirties. They raised six kids, worked hard to provide for their family, and sacrificed so much for us every day. They were my primary caregivers after I was shot and did everything they could to make my life easier. My dad was also my mom's caregiver when she was sick; he even managed to work a part-time job during that time to help pay for her medications. My parents defined selflessness. I'm so glad I paid attention to their example. I could never be to others what they were to me, but they certainly gave me a ridiculously high standard to strive for.

*****

That's my 273-page memoir condensed into a few thousand words. I have many more stories to share with you in this book, most of which you will not find in my memoir. As you read my real-life examples of each principle in action, think about your life and how the principles can be applied to everything you say and do each day. Also understand that you're not going to ace this—ever. None of us are, because we aren't perfect beings. But if we continually put forth the effort to listen, to empathize, to forgive, to laugh, to be optimistic, and to be kind, the love and peace will steadily flow—from our hearts and into the lives of those we encounter—drowning all the hate and negativity in their path. It really is a beautiful image when you think about it, one that together we can bring to life.

Take Action!
Learn Someone Else's Story

Activity #1: Pair with someone you do not know very well (teachers may want to assign the pairings so that participants are not tempted to pair with friends). Share unknown tidbits about your lives with each other. Don't share deep secrets or anything embarrassing—just fun facts that will give you both a peek into each other's stories. Maybe you lived in a different state. Maybe you are a good dancer or juggler or basketball player. Maybe you are friends with or have met a celebrity. Maybe you have a unique hobby.

After sharing those fun facts, ask each other two questions about each one. For example, if the person tells you she is a good dancer, you might ask her what kind of music she likes to dance to and if she has a dream of dancing professionally. If her answers lead you to want to ask more questions and she is comfortable answering more questions, then ask them. Let the discussion flow where it may.

When you are finished, tell the other person what you have learned about them. Are you surprised about the knowledge you have gained? How has your perspective of that person changed? If you would like to continue this exercise, switch partners and share fun facts that are different from what you just shared with your previous partners.

Activity #2: Work with a partner to create a superhero based on what you have learned about each other in the activity above. This will be one superhero—a combination of both of your stories. You can draw this superhero using life-size bulletin board paper or simple construction paper. Partners will then share their superhero with the class. Each partner will discuss the *other* partner's contributions to the characteristics of the superhero.

Activity #3: This activity would work best in a small group of maybe four or five people. Each person should write down three statements about themselves: two that are true and one that is not true. Each person will then read all three statements to the group, and the group has to guess which one is not true. The purpose of this is to not only learn more about each other, but to create a discussion. For example, if someone writes that broccoli is her favorite vegetable and that is not true, the group can ask her what her favorite vegetable really is, or if she has ever tasted broccoli, or what it would take for her to taste it. That could cause another person to share their experience with broccoli. See how much more you can learn about each other through this discussion.

Activity #4: For high school students, show the beginning of the 1985 film *The Breakfast Club,* when the five students in detention don't know each other. Then, show the clip toward the end of the movie when they are gathered in a circle telling each other their stories. Discuss how they came to respect each other at the end of the movie despite being five very different people.

Journal Entry: In general (not specific to your partner), what have you learned by recognizing that everyone has a story different from yours? How can showing a genuine interest in others change your life for the better?

Listen

"When people talk, listen completely. Most people never listen."
– Ernest Hemingway

O NE OF MY FAVORITE sayings is, "Talk is cheap, because the supply is greater than the demand." I don't know who said it first, but he or she must have had a brilliant mind. It is a phrase that should be plastered everywhere to remind us of the importance and value of listening to each other.

Listening, in my opinion, is a lost art. Fewer and fewer people today are very good at it, which can lead to communication breakdowns and all sorts of problems in relationships, school, and business. Sure, we *hear* people's words all day and every day, but do we really *listen* to those words? Do we show interest in what someone is saying? Try to understand them? Learn from them? Let them speak before we respond?

Today's technology is fantastic. I love my computer, my cell phone, and my ability to communicate using text and social media, and I know many kids today have never known life without any of it. But I see a growing and dangerous imbalance between technology and face-to-face human contact. Yes, technology can save a lot of time and money, but it cannot replace the value and emotions of in-person interaction. When we need to (or should) have a meaningful conversation with someone, many of us don't know how or simply don't want to because we are so used to communicating from behind our gadgets. That deficiency can lead to misunderstandings, false accusations, hurt feelings, relationship breakups, or even a lack of life-or-death help for somebody who simply needs someone to listen to them at a critical time.

How often have you tried to have a conversation with a friend who is sitting right next to you—in school, in the car, in a restaurant—but her eyes and attention are focused on her phone instead of you? Frustrating, isn't it? How often have you tried to have a discussion with someone via text or on social media, only to have it become an argument because one or both of you are more concerned about typing what you want to say next rather than listening to and trying to understand each other's perspective? I even know some people who refuse to answer their phone when it rings, even if they know who is calling. "Why can't you just text?" the person will argue. Um, because I need you to truly listen to me, not coldly respond to my texts with LOLs and emojis while you're distracted by a video you're watching of a three-legged goat bouncing on a trampoline with a one-eared rabbit.

The evolution of television is a great example of how listening skills have devolved. Many years ago, probably before your time, there were quality, wholesome TV shows such as *The Andy Griffith Show, Leave it to Beaver, Happy Days, Family Matters,* and *Full House.* The dads and/or moms on those shows always provided sound advice to their children, but only after carefully and attentively listening to what their children had to say.

Compare those to the countless reality and talk shows that flood channels today. When I turn on just about anything on VH1, MTV, E!, or ESPN, for example, my head nearly explodes! The shows feature multiple people yelling over each other trying to make their voices heard rather than listening to those with whom they are supposed to be conversing. When they are all finally silenced (it usually takes a commercial to do that), none of them know what anybody else has said, and nothing has been solved or accomplished. So they start the madness all over again in the next segment. It's easy to see why there is so much dysfunction in those families.

Have you ever seen an episode of *Keeping Up with the Kardashians?* Gosh, I hope your answer is no. But, if you have, you know that their lives are a dramatic mess filled with countless problems and finger-pointing. Many of their issues in each episode start because everybody is caught up in themselves instead of trying to listen to each other. And then, after watching a segment of their bickering, the show cuts to a segment in which one of the cast members talks directly into the camera, explaining their side of what we just watched. I have always wondered, *Why are they talking into a camera instead of conversing with the person they are griping about on camera?* I guess if they did that, there would be less drama, which would mean no show...which is quite sad.

I know to some people this is entertaining television. Unfortunately, many youth (and even adults) are influenced by it to the extent that they think it is acceptable everyday behavior. They mimic it in their own lives, even in the smallest of ways, and the rage from person to person spreads.

*****

I have read numerous publications on how to be a good listener. They offer several very good ideas, such as making good eye contact, leaning in toward the person who is speaking so your body language shows you're listening, and not being distracted by your phone. But the best and most encompassing tip of all is probably the simplest one of all: keep your mouth closed and your attention focused the speaker.

I have found through my work that many kids today don't necessarily want advice; they just want to be heard. They long to tell their story to someone who will listen, who will respect their views, who will be empathetic. I have also found that many of them don't trust they will be able to find adults who will listen without injecting their two cents, which may be why many kids clam up around their parents. Kids today are often so worried about being judged by someone that they choose to keep their problems to themselves, which can be self-destructive and hurt others. This is why many youth end up in my care at day treatment.

When Michael was bullied, he had no faith that anybody, including teachers and administrators, would listen to him. Read this brief exchange between him and Detective Carl Baker of the McCracken County Sheriff's Department. This conversation (a fraction of the entire conversation they had, which is published in my memoir) occurred just a couple hours after the shooting, so it's as raw as it could be. Michael was crying while telling Detective Baker about a boy who had been bullying him:

Det. Baker: "Was this like an everyday thing?"

Michael: "Yeah, like sometimes, in ICP, which is science, I would say something like telling him to be quiet or something 'cause he was always making fun of me. When we got out of the class he would hit me, just like right in the head for no reason."

Det. Baker: "Why would he do that? Did he ever tell you why he did it? Hit you with his fist? Was it always his fist or did he use something else?"

Michael: "Sometimes he would kick me in the shin."

Det. Baker: "Did you tell teachers?"

Michael: "Uh, they don't do much."

Did you notice that each question asked by Det. Baker was in direct response to what Michael said? And did you notice that he never interrupted Michael? Nor did he judge anything Michael said. This was likely the first time in a very long time that any person had truly listened to Michael. Unfortunately, the damage had already been done.

I loved my teachers, principal, and the all of the administrators and staff at Heath. They will always be heroes to me. But I wonder how evident it was to kids like Michael that they were willing to listen. Why did Michael, who was being physically, mentally, and emotionally tormented day in and day out by other students, tolerate that abuse rather than tell someone about it? There was obviously a disconnection there that nobody realized, one that many schools and states are still trying to fix today with anti-bullying policies and laws. Policies and laws can and do help, but we should listen and pay more attention to each other because we want to, because we want a world of love and peace, because we know everyone has a story different from ours and may need our help—not because a governing body has ordered us to.

Being kind shouldn't have to be legislated.

Many teachers believe they are in the speaking or lecturing business, but the best educators will tell you that listening is what matters. When I talked to Michael in prison, he said he wished he had spoken up more and had sought help. Instead, he held everything in because he didn't feel comfortable confiding in anybody, including his own family and friends. With suicides at rates higher than we've ever seen, especially among teens and our brave military personnel, it is so important to listen to each other and to let others know that we are willing to listen. Only then will we be able to effectively help someone.

*****

One of the most memorable and personally satisfying listening moments of my speaking career happened when I was giving a talk at a large middle school in Kentucky. The gymnasium was packed wall to wall with hundreds of students in grades six, seven, and eight, and from the district's day treatment center. There was a buzz in the air the entire time. My talk lasted roughly forty-five minutes, and the kids were riveted. Usually when I get to the thirty- or forty-minute mark, especially with such a large group, I'll see some students get fidgety. (I can totally empathize; I recall when I was in school that many speakers went on *way* too long.) But, for whatever reason, I had these students' full attention from beginning to end. It was a beautiful thing.

But it got even better.

After I had finished my talk, and as one of the administrators was instructing the students on how they would file out and return to their classrooms, a young boy with a glimmer of a smile on his face walked toward me. I knew nothing about him. Not his name, grade, age, or why he was coming my way. As I would later be told, just the fact that he was voluntarily coming to speak with me was a monumental moment—to him, to his teachers, and even to some other students.

The boy, as I would eventually learn, was a student in their day treatment center. He had been there for a long time because of several difficult issues he had faced at home and in school, including bullying. Each day, from the time he would arrive at the center to the time he would leave to return home, he wouldn't speak. Teachers had tried everything possible, and believe me when I say that day treatment center teachers have more creative ideas to reach students than one can imagine. But this boy wouldn't budge—until now.

As he courageously approached me, a friend of mine who had accompanied me to my talk heard a teacher gasp and say to another teacher, "Oh my gosh, look!" Other teachers and even some students had the same reaction. You could hear a hushed yet excited murmur throughout the gym. When the boy got to me, he introduced himself.

"Thank you for coming to speak," he said. "I really liked it."

He said my talk had helped him a lot, and he told me in confidence why it meant so much. I thanked him and asked him a couple simple questions, like what grade he was in and where he was from, but I primarily listened. I didn't offer advice or try to solve any of his problems; I could tell he didn't want that. He just wanted to be heard, and he felt now was the time to speak. Our conversation didn't last more than a minute or two, but as I would later learn, it was one of the best moments that any of his teachers had witnessed in his recent life.

There are three examples in this story of the power of listening.

The first is that he listened to my talk. I have no doubt that the day treatment staff had tried just about everything to get him to open up. I would be willing to bet that none of it worked not because of them, but because he had shut them out and refused to listen. It's possible that he looked at them simply as mainstream classroom teachers, no different than the ones he had had in his school prior to day treatment, and he had just made up his mind that he wasn't going to talk to a teacher. Maybe it was the day treatment setting that kept him quiet, which can be intimidating with so many troubled students in one place. Or maybe he'd given up hope that he would ever get better and felt that talking about his problems with anyone at school wasn't going to help.

But why me?

There are several possibilities. It could have been because I was in a wheelchair and he recognized that, despite my vulnerability, I was speaking up and telling my story. It could be that he didn't see me as a teacher or counselor, as I am in my regular job, but as an outsider who came in to inspire and help students like him. Or maybe there was something specific I said during my talk that struck a chord with him, something that made him believe he could trust me. Maybe it was a bit of all three. Whatever it was, it happened only because he had listened to me. He paid attention rather than shutting me out and letting his mind wander.

Trust that there is *always* someone who will truly listen to you, who *wants* to listen to you. I have no doubt that all of his teachers would have loved for him to confide in them, and they likely tried multiple times to get him to, but for whatever reason he didn't feel comfortable enough to do it. If you feel that way about those around you, that's okay, but do not use it as an excuse to give up finding that person you feel is right for you. Believe me when I say that he or she is definitely out there, and probably much closer than you think. When all hope seems lost, take a calculated risk and put your trust in someone. I think you will be shocked to find how many people are willing to help you and really do care about you.

The second example is that *I* listened to *him*, and without judgment. Remember, I had no idea who he was. I didn't know his story. I didn't know that he hadn't spoken to anybody in a long time. I didn't even know he was in day treatment. He could have been the smartest kid and best athlete in the middle school with no personal issues at all as far as I knew. But when he walked down to speak to me, none of that mattered to me. What mattered was that a student went out of his way to introduce himself and thank me for being there. I appreciated him and thought only the best of him, no matter what triggered him to come down or what his story was. There was a generous amount of love flowing between us during our brief meeting, all of it mutually unconditional.

A third example is that his teachers "listened" to the encounter between him and me. They didn't listen in the literal sense—they were too far away to hear what he and I were talking about—but they listened with their eyes by paying full attention to our positive body language toward one another and the fact that he had made the effort to come down from the bleachers to talk to me. What the teachers saw likely gave them some additional hope that they could still reach him and help him overcome his many obstacles.

That's the power of listening. It can be life-changing.

*****

We once had two girls in day treatment who had anger issues. And when I say "anger issues," I mean serious stuff. All it took was for someone to look at them or say something to them in a way the girls didn't like for them to turn violent. You may attend a school where this kind of thing is unimaginable, which is good for you and something you should be grateful for, but know that it's not that unusual in many schools across the country.

Interestingly enough, not only did these girls have no previous problems with each other, but they didn't even know each other despite going to the same school. Other kids in their school, however, knew how to push their buttons and make them mad, and they thought it would be funny to try to pit the girls against each other.

One day, some students decided to see if they could make the two girls fight each other. They first went to Girl A and told her that Girl B was saying some nasty things about the way she was dressed. With Girl A instantly and noticeably livid, the kids quickly rushed over to Girl B and told her that Girl A had been saying some bad things about her and wanted to fight her. Sure enough, within minutes, the fight was on. After administrators stepped in to break it up before it got out of hand, we spoke to the girls about why they were fighting. It was the first time they'd actually listened to each other, and it was when they'd learned the truth: they had been set up. Neither one had a single unkind word to say about the other.

The obvious problem in this situation was the kids who lied to both girls to get them to fight. When creating a fight between two people is not only acceptable but enjoyable to people, there are likely serious problems in their home lives. Their attitudes are what we are all up against in our effort to promote love and peace. They are the ones who most need to learn about listening, empathy, and kindness. Changing their ways is quite the task, but with the reward so great, it is why I do what I do and why I will never give up on any child.

The girls also had to share blame for what had happened. They were the ones who ultimately chose to resort to physical violence based purely on speculation. Once we got the girls together to listen to each other, they realized that they had no problems with each other, and they even had some positive things in common. Unfortunately, they had chosen to believe

27

the negatives without knowing the other one's story or without listening to the other one, which led to the fight.

When you choose to assume the worst about someone or believe rumors rather than seek the truth, you are only fueling the fire of negativity. It's a choice that could lead you to do or say something you will regret, something that could result in devastating consequences for you and those around you.

*****

The first time I recall *really* listening as a teenager was when I was in the hospital about a week after the shooting. I had been in pretty good spirits at that time because I had just been moved out of intensive care and into a regular room. I felt like I was ready to take on my life with paralysis—though I admit that I did have some difficult moments. It wasn't any one particular day or event that would put me in a gloomy mood. When you're lying in a hospital where the most exciting thing happening is a nurse coming in to draw blood, there is little to do but think. And when you think about how you will not be able to control at least half of your body ever again, it's easy to fall into bouts of depression.

That's what happened to me.

As positive of a person as I was even then, I couldn't help but wonder at times how I was going to live this new life. How was I going to maneuver a wheelchair? How would I get up or down steps? How was I going to learn how to drive? Was that even a possibility anymore? What boy is ever going to like me now? Who would want to marry me? Was my dream of making it in the WNBA over? Okay, I was horrible at basketball, so that wasn't really my dream. But, seriously, would I be able to have children? Could I go to college? Could I work? Who would hire a girl in a wheelchair?

My mom was at my side in the hospital every day. My dad, my sister Christie, and others in my family gave her some relief, so I was never alone. But it was my mom who was there the most and the one who could sense when I was struggling emotionally, despite the fact that I tried not to show it. One day, when she knew I needed a pick-me-up, she started reading me letters. Those hundreds and hundreds of letters I said that I had received each day from around the world for weeks—that was no exaggeration. I received as many as six hundred in one day, not to mention a ridiculous number of packages and gifts.

So Mom opened the letters, one by one, and read them out loud. I'm ashamed to say that I wasn't initially thrilled about having to lie there and hear her read what people I didn't know had to say; I was just too depressed. But she gave me no choice, and I'm glad she didn't. My mind wandered as she read an initial batch of them, but with nowhere to go and knowing she wasn't going to stop, I began to actually listen.

Dear Missy,

You don't know me, but you better believe that you and your entire family are in my prayers. I received an email from a friend of mine in Birmingham, AL that told me all about your situation. I live in Auburn, AL and am a freshman at Auburn University. Your attitude toward the boy that shot you should be an encouragement to everyone. I know it is to me!

And then there was this one that made me laugh for the first time in a while:

Dear Missy,
I am so sorry that little boy got possed (I think that was supposed to be "possessed") *by Satan my dad said. There's a short kid in my school and everybody loves him, he's my friend and so are you!*

Was he calling me short? Ha-ha! I'm pretty sure that's not what he meant. (Just for the record: I may only be 4 feet 1 inch tall sitting in my wheelchair, but I am 5 feet 7 inches tall stretched from head to toe.)

Every letter was just like those—beautiful, heartfelt, innocent, funny, encouraging. When I listened to and processed them, I knew that I wasn't in this alone. While the entire world was focused on Paducah, and even though I think I sort of knew that, I didn't know to what extent because I wasn't on the outside seeing what other people were seeing or talking with others about the shooting. I was isolated. The magnitude of the impact of what Michael did was a little lost on me, but those thousands of letters gave me a new perspective.

I reflected long and hard about the letter from the girl in Auburn. Why did she take time to write to me? She lived more than four hundred miles away, didn't know me, had a busy college life—yet she stopped her world to handwrite a letter to someone she had never met, not even knowing if I would actually receive it and read it. Who does that? It took me some time to understand who, but I eventually realized it was the type of person who was kind, who attentively read my story, and who had empathized with my plight to the extent that she felt compelled to reach out to me. It made me feel good, and it probably made her feel good, too. It was a simple gesture of love that took relatively little time, but had an impact so huge that I am still talking about it twenty years later.

I obviously couldn't respond to every letter I had received, but to her, to the boy who was sorry that Michael "got possed," and to the thousands of others who reached out to me, please know that I did listen to your words, and they made all the difference at just the right time. You listened to my story, you believed in me, and that helped me believe in myself.

*****

After being in the hospital for a couple of months, I was transferred to Cardinal Hill in Lexington, Kentucky, to begin some serious rehabilitation. I was the youngest person there among roughly fifteen other patients, most of who were in wheelchairs like me.

One patient I vividly recall was in his forties. He had been struck by a falling tree and was paralyzed like me. Aside from our ages, there was one huge difference between us: our attitudes. I don't think I had ever met anyone more negative. No matter what anyone said or did, he managed to find the worst in it. You could have brought him the perfect chocolate ice cream cone and he would have complained that it was too cold, too hard, too creamy, too chocolaty, not chocolaty enough, whatever. Someone to probably avoid, right? Well, a lot of the other patients did, but I decided to risk taking the opposite approach and lend him an ear.

I introduced myself with a warm smile, and I'll admit that being a young country girl with a bit of a southern accent was probably to my advantage (not a whole lot there to be intimidated about, right?). I didn't ask him just about his injury, but about his life. He said he had a wife and child who loved him very much and were determined to help him recover. I shared my story with him when he asked, which helped him realize that we had the same injuries and he wasn't alone in what he was experiencing.

We talked a little each day, though I let him do most of the talking. After a few days, I bought him a stress ball that he could squeeze whenever he felt angry about something, and I don't think I'd ever seen a stress ball get such a workout. It was not only meant to help him relieve tension, but to remind him that I cared about him.

After a week or two we had become good friends, and we looked forward to conversing each day. I had convinced him that while he may have felt that his life was over, it wasn't; it was just different. He acknowledged my efforts in the most gracious of ways when he stopped my mom in the hall one day as she was walking toward my room to visit me. He told her that I had helped him so much simply by showing an interest in him and his well-being. From my perspective, I hadn't done a whole lot. In the simplest terms, I just listened to him. From his perspective, though, it was life-changing.

I don't know what happened to him after we parted ways at Cardinal Hill. I hope that he is still doing well today, and I hope the joy I was able to bring him by listening is a gift that he's passed on to others.

*****

On December 16, 1998, more than a year after the shooting, Michael appeared in McCracken County Circuit Court for his sentencing. Before the sentencing, Judge Jeff Hines gave anyone who was victimized by Michael's actions the opportunity to speak to the court.

I don't recall Judge Hines stating any rules for how this would proceed, but it was understood that we would each take a turn to talk at the podium, and Michael and his attorney would not be allowed to speak. This wasn't going to be a back-and-forth exchange. We were going to talk, and he was going to listen—or at least hear our words.

Nine of us spoke. A couple people, like my friend Kelly Hard who was shot in the back, yelled at Michael with every ounce of energy she had. She told him he should be put to death for what he did, and she questioned his value of life. Others, especially parents of the girls who died, were relatively calm as they fought back tears to say what they wanted to say. It was difficult to tell if Michael was really listening. He kept his head down as people spoke until Stephen Keene, the brother of shooting victim Craig Keene, addressed Michael for two minutes.

"My statement is not specifically for this court. It is for that young man sitting right there. Michael, I watched you gun down three girls and murder them. I watched you shoot my brother and try to kill him and five other people. If I have to watch that—you look at me right now."

Michael looked up at him, the first time he'd looked up at anybody. Stephen continued.

"You know, I don't understand what your whole point is. What would drive somebody to do this man? Respond!" Michael continued to look at him, but didn't speak. "I wish it was that easy," Stephen said. "I wish I couldn't respond to anything. I wish it was that easy for me."

My sister, Mandy, spoke after Stephen, and I followed her. Having watched Michael with his head down as most people spoke versus keeping his head up when Stephen spoke, I decided to take a page from Stephen's book.

"I want Michael to look at me," I said. He did, and he did not take his eyes off of me until I was finished.

"Alright—I want to tell you that I'm paralyzed. I'm paralyzed from my chest right here down. And I spent five months in the hospital, and I still struggle. And I feel really helpless. I can't do things like I used to. I can't do things on my own like I used to. I can't go to the bathroom like regular people. It's hard to get dressed. I see people running around doing stuff like everybody else, and I can't really do it because I'm stuck to my chair. They tell me that I'll never walk again. I think I will, though. But if God doesn't want me to walk, that's okay. And I just wanted you to know because I have to live with it every day now.

"And I don't know why you did this to me and everybody else, but I know that I'm never going to forget it because I see it every day in my mind. But I don't have any hard feelings toward you. I'm just upset that this happened and I'm upset that everything had to go this way, but I can live this way. It's going to be hard, but I can do it. That's really all I had to say."

When I met with Michael in prison in 2007, he told me that he remembered the sentencing. He said he could not recall what everybody had said to him when they spoke, but he said he did remember everything that I had said. There is no question in my mind that he heard everyone's words that day, but only listened to some of them. Telling him to look at me as I spoke no doubt focused his attention on me and forced him to listen.

*****

A final story regarding listening that I would like to share is a short and simple one about a recent talk I gave at a public high school in southern Illinois. A social worker at the school had invited me to speak after hearing about me from a colleague; it was the first time I had ever visited this school. The talk went very well, and the students gave me a wonderful ovation when it was finished. I will say that while I know all of the applause I have received at my engagements over the years has been sincere, I don't always know exactly how well or to how many students my message resonated. I was pretty confident these students took my message to heart, but it wasn't until the next morning when that feeling was confirmed.

I woke up to get ready for work and checked my phone. There was a text message from the social worker. Attached to her message was a photo she had just taken of about a dozen students. They were standing in a prayer circle in their school lobby, something they had decided to start that morning and vowed to do each day after listening to me speak the previous day.

I was moved to tears. I certainly had not told them they should start one; they did it completely on their own. In fact, the prayer circle is never more than a brief mention during my talks, a simple fact I state at the start when I explain what happened the morning of the shooting. But because they had listened intently to my talk, they were able to open their minds to ideas they could implement at their school that could make it a friendlier, more inviting, and more loving environment. It was truly an honor that they would do something like that—to me and to all of us at Heath who were in that prayer circle two decades earlier.

*****

The best feature about listening is that nothing special is required to do it. You don't need a college degree or certified training or an app. You don't have to be a certain age or have had specific experiences in life. Heck, you don't even have to personally know the person you're listening to. It can be anyone from a close friend to your waiter at a restaurant to a homeless person on the street. It can be anybody, anywhere, anytime. All that is required of you is that you block out all potential distractions, open your ears, stay silent, and be present for the person. Not only can it change someone's life, it can greatly enrich your own life.

Take Action!
Listen

ℒ

Activity #1: Listening to others is an active endeavor. In a group of four or five people, use what you have learned about being a good listener to develop an infographic (a diagram or chart) that shows a process of how to effectively listen to another person. For example, Step 1 of your infographic may be to look at the speaker. Step 2 may be to have an open mind. Step 3 may be to listen carefully to each word that is spoken. And so on. Show these and additional steps through your diagram or chart.

After creating the infographic, sit in a circle with your group. Each person should take a turn completing the phrase: "If you knew my story, you would know that…" Again, these do not have to be deep secrets; only say what you are comfortable saying. Talk for about twenty to thirty seconds, giving some details about your story. Each person listening should be mindful of the listening steps they just created in the infographic. After everyone has spoken, each person should take a turn talking about what they have just learned about another person in the group, showing the results of their listening skills.

Activity #2: Instead of, or in addition to, saying what you have learned about another person in the group, create a rap song about what you have learned about another person and perform it in front of the group or class. You can be creative with your lyrics, but they should be clear evidence of how well you listened to the person tell his or her story.

Activity #3: Write, or perform in front of your class, a public service announcement or short skit that shows the actions and importance of listening. Keep in mind how you know when someone is listening to you and how that makes you feel.

Journal Entry: Why is actively listening to others important? How can this skill/practice improve your life? (Think of it in terms of various dimensions, such as family, friends, school, work, your future career, sports, music, etc.)

Empathize

"Have a heart that never hardens, and a temper that never tires,
and a touch that never hurts."
– Charles Dickens

W E HAD A FIFTEEN-year-old boy in day treatment who other kids labeled as "weird." He didn't take good care of himself. He wore the same clothes each day. He rarely showered. He struggled to interact with anyone in a "normal" way. At lunch in the cafeteria, he ate whatever food he could get his hands on. One time he chugged so much milk that he vomited. Seriously, some kids looked forward to watching him eat each day more than they did eating their own lunches.

The first reactions his classmates had to anything he did was, "What is wrong with him?" and "Why is he like that?" Some of them teased him and made fun of him. They contributed to the destruction of his self-esteem.

Another counselor and I worked with him to try to figure out the root cause of his behaviors, and the answers we found easily explained everything. As you read what we discovered, try your hardest to put yourself in his shoes. In other words, imagine the person I am describing is you.

The boy's mother had died soon after he was born. He had no memory of her. The only memento he had was a lone picture of her someone in his family had given to him. He was raised by his father, who abused him. They were homeless for much of the boy's life. That explained why he struggled to interact with other people—he simply didn't trust anyone after what his own dad had done to him. It also explained why he ate and drank so much at school. That food was likely the only food he would have access to all day. He knew that once he left school, his stomach would be empty until he returned the next morning. On weekends, he probably had nothing.

After his dad was arrested and imprisoned, the boy went to live with his grandparents. While they loved their grandson, they were an elderly disabled couple who were barely able to make ends meet. One day, I saw the boy walking home from the grocery store carrying groceries that his grandparents couldn't get on their own because of their disabilities. That helped explain his poor hygiene. He hadn't taken care of himself not only because his father had never taught him how, but because he felt obligated to put his grandparents' needs ahead of his own. Whatever money they sent with him to the store went toward food or things his grandparents needed for their own health.

When we learned all of this, we did everything we could to assist him. We bought him a toothbrush, toothpaste, soap, deodorant, and shampoo. We took his clothes to our own homes and washed them. We helped his family secure food. And we taught him some simple ways to take care of himself and still take care of his grandparents. The bullying eventually stopped, and as kids in school gradually learned a little bit about his story as his appearance and behavior improved, their attitudes toward him changed for the better.

I just provided you a condensed version of his story, but hopefully enough to give you a sense of what his life was like, and why. Did you find it admirable that this "weird" kid who couldn't interact with anybody at school took care of his grandparents and selflessly put them ahead of himself? Did you think differently of him once you realized why he drank and ate as much as he did? Did you try to picture yourself being in his position—homeless, dirty, hungry, abused, parentless, all as a young teenager? Rather than agree that he is "weird," did you instead feel a desire to help him?

If the answers to those questions are "yes," then congratulations! You are an empathetic person, which is what the world so desperately needs right now.

*****

Simply defined, empathy is putting yourself in another person's shoes. It's having an open mind and seeing the world from their perspective. It's immersing yourself into their story—seeing what they see, hearing what they hear, feeling their pain and suffering, experiencing their emotions. An empathetic person is a compassionate person who listens, who is tolerant of any differences. Author Eric Harvey said, "Remember that I'm Human. Before you judge me or decide how you'll deal with me, walk awhile in my shoes. If you do, I think you'll find with more understanding we can meet in the middle and walk the rest of the way together."

To meet in the middle, we have to be willing to empathize rather than push our views on or make rash judgments about others. Rather than judging a kid based on how he looks or behaves, meet him in the middle by learning his story, then walk with him from that point forward, as a friend or even just an acquaintance, but not as someone who is going to callously tear him down at every turn. When we can empathize, we can love. When we can empathize, we can bring peace to others and to their situations.

Empathizing with someone is a challenge. We are all born and raised in certain environments, with certain beliefs, with certain ways of doing things. Trying to put ourselves in the shoes of someone with whom we are unfamiliar or whose beliefs directly conflict with ours can be difficult. But being empathetic doesn't necessarily mean we have to agree with someone. It simply shows that we are making an effort to understand their perspective, which is different from ours because their story is different from ours. We are educating ourselves while also becoming more tolerant and compassionate in the process. We are growing as people, preparing ourselves for future encounters with others in school, at work, or in our neighborhoods.

The lack of empathy today can be witnessed in many places, but maybe none more than on social media. Social media opens the door for us to be empathetic, but many people choose to go the opposite direction—they slam that door shut, isolate themselves behind their phones or computers, and post whatever they want about whomever they want without any concern for how their comments will affect anybody.

If you watched Super Bowl LI in February of 2017 between New England and Atlanta, you probably saw Lady Gaga's halftime show. I like her music, and I also like that she supports a lot of wonderful causes, including anti-bullying efforts. Unfortunately, it took people just seconds after the conclusion of her Super Bowl performance to bully her on social media.

While I saw her that evening as a woman who courageously sang, danced, and did some spectacular acrobatic moves in front of a live television audience of more than one hundred million people, some of those people chose to focus on her exposed midriff during part of the performance and body shame her. One person tweeted that he was trying to enjoy the show, but he was "distracted by the flab on her stomach swinging around." Another person said, "Lady Gaga needs to do some crunches if she wants to show her flabby belly."

I have no idea what the story could be of people who, instead of reaching for the nacho dip at halftime like most football fans, reach for their phones to post nasty messages to the world about a woman they don't know, someone who just successfully did something they could never do. But, unfortunately, that's what a lot of people use social media for, whether it be to put down a celebrity or even a friend.

There is a guy in Ohio I follow on Facebook named Mike Gershe who runs a nonprofit organization called The Magic of Life, which educates people on the dangers of drinking and driving. Mike posted a comment after the 2016 U.S. presidential election about how several of our politicians, both Democrats and Republicans, were bullying each other, and that if they wanted everyday citizens in this country to come together and promote peace and love, the politicians needed to lead by example. Mike is not a confrontational person in the least; his post was very thoughtful and nonpartisan. Not surprisingly, it didn't take long for people to comment and take politically-driven shots at him and each other, blaming the "other party" for the negativity. After Mike decided he had had enough of the pessimism and deleted the post, he received a private message from one of his followers whom he didn't even know.

"You're a loser," she said. "When you're challenged you run. What happened to your bullying post? Stop hiding behind your mother's death by a drunk driver so many years ago and get on with your life. You aren't here to avenge your mother's death. Live your life, move forward."

What I haven't told you yet about Mike is that when he was a baby, he and his family were hit by a drunk driver. His mother was killed, and Mike had every bone in his fragile, infant body broken. How he survived will always be a mystery. After Mike graduated from college, he started his nonprofit in memory of his mother. He speaks nationwide and has reached tens of thousands of youth and adults, including in schools, on military bases, and in jails.

Now that you know his story, let's break down that message he received:

First, calling him a loser is immature by any standard and doesn't deserve any more attention.

Second, he didn't "run" by deleting his post; it was simply becoming too hostile, to the point that he didn't want the hate that was spewing to continue on his page or possibly spill onto another one.

Third, he has never hid behind his mother's death or tried to "avenge" her death. He doesn't even know if the drunk driver who hit them is still alive, nor does he really care at this stage in his life.

And fourth, he has "moved forward" with his life in a fabulous way with the creation and success of his organization.

Mike took the high road and shared all of this information with this woman in a very classy manner, but she never responded. She disappeared from among his followers and was never heard from again. It's obvious that empathy was not much of a component of her life. Sadly, this type of behavior on social media is becoming far too common.

Put yourself in Mike's shoes for a moment. Imagine if the crash he was in had happened to you and your mom, or to you and your dad, or to you and whoever your guardian may be. Imagine having grown up without that person in your life. Can you picture it? Sure you can. Do you *want* to picture it? Of course not. It's not pleasant to think about. But it's what we need to make ourselves do to truly feel compassion for others. It's what we need to do to understand who they are. We don't need to dwell on it, but we need to do it to the extent that we can fully appreciate their story. To empathize with someone, we need to remove ourselves from our comfort zone and put ourselves into that person's space. I can assure you that if the woman who had sent him that message had put her energy into being empathetic toward Mike, she never would have sent such a message.

I think it would be fantastic if, just before we are about to post something on a social media site, the site would flash a simple sentence that says: "Think before you post this." Too often we are so anxious to post a comment or photo or video as soon as it happens that we don't think about whom it may affect in a negative way. Sometimes I see people post photos of car accidents they've driven past and I ask myself, "Why? If that were you in the accident, would you like strangers taking photos and sharing them with the world? What good will come from you posting these?" Or I see someone post a photo they secretly took on the street or at the beach of someone they don't know and they body shame that person or make fun of the way she was dressed. Again…why?

Take a moment to empathize before you post anything. If it is negative in any way, think twice about posting it. And if your head or your heart are urging you not to do it, then absolutely don't do it. What you don't post will not be missed by anybody.

*****

Several years ago I was invited by a friend to attend one of her church's Sunday services. Though I already belonged to a church, I have always been open to learning about other faiths, so I accepted her invitation. What specifically intrigued me about her invitation was that she called her service "a healing service." My simple interpretation was that it was a service where they pray for people who are looking for healing in some way, similar to what we do in my church. Being in a wheelchair and having never given up hope that I still might walk one day, I was thrilled to let people at another church share in that hope.

I found a cozy spot in the back of the church when I arrived to try to lay low and just take in the service from a distance. Being a young person in a wheelchair often attracts attention, and that was the last thing I wanted to do in this unfamiliar place. The service began with general prayers—nothing out of the ordinary. Then they called a gentleman up to the front who had been sick. Once he was up there, several people formed a circle around him. I could see that each of them was touching the man, giving him a blessing.

Well, that's a bit different, I thought to myself. But it was nothing compared to what was about to happen.

After each person blessed him, they all held hands...and then they began speaking in tongues! The longer they prayed for him, the louder they became. I had no idea what they were saying, but it seemed to me, by the intensity of their words, that they weren't just praying for him to heal—they were praying for him to heal right then and there! They wanted an instant miracle! I had never witnessed something like this. There was nothing wrong with it—if they wanted to give it a shot, more power to them—it was just unlike anything I had ever seen before.

When they were finished praying for the man, who claimed to have felt some healing, my friend turned to me.

"Missy," she said with a smile. "You want to try?"

Uhhhhhhh...

Before I could respond, all eyes in the church were locked on me as my friend eagerly waved at me to come up front. So much for lying low. My nerves were telling me to politely say "No thank you, I'm good," but since I was an invited guest, I felt that would be rude, so I tentatively wheeled my way to the front. Just as they did with the man before me, several people formed a circle around me, and each of them touched me with a blessing. Then came the tongues.

I'm not going to sugarcoat it: when I'm surrounded by a bunch of people I don't know who are touching me and saying words I don't understand in an effort to try to instantly heal me, something that some of the country's best doctors have never been able to do for me, it's a little scary and uncomfortable. But I tried to put myself in their shoes and keep an open mind. Their intentions were good, and by witnessing what they had done with the first person, I knew what to expect. I also knew that my friend had invited me to try to help me, not to scare me; she wasn't going to put me in a bad situation. There is a difference between feeling uncomfortable and feeling threatened. I felt uncomfortable because this was a new experience for me, but by having an open mind as I assessed the situation and viewed it from their perspective, I never felt threatened by what they were doing.

After several minutes, the touching and talking in tongues stopped. They all looked at me with what I would describe as restrained enthusiasm; it was obvious we weren't finished. They were expecting something big to happen. I had no idea just how big.

"Missy, we would like you to get up and walk now," one of the people said matter-of-factly.

Whoooooooa! You want me to what?

Fortunately, I didn't blurt that reaction out loud, but I'm pretty sure my eyes about popped out of my head. I looked at my friend, who was nodding and smiling ear to ear with the rest of them, encouraging me to give it a shot. *Oh my gosh, what do I do?* My immediate reaction was that I needed to figure out a way to make like Houdini and disappear. But the empathetic me, who knew their intentions were good, told me to stay calm and find a better way out of it.

As much as I appreciated what they were trying to do, I touched my legs with my hands to confirm what I already knew—I couldn't feel them, which meant my physical status hadn't changed. I was still paralyzed. I hadn't walked in more than a decade, and there was no way I would be able to walk now.

A couple of them stepped to either side of me, ready to lift me by my arms, but I had to stop them. My legs were telling me exactly what was going to happen: I was going to fall to the floor like a wet noodle and likely drag them down with me, risking injury to all of us. It wasn't going to be a pretty sight. Yes, it would have made a hysterical YouTube video, but I didn't want that, either.

"You know, I would rather not do that," I said as respectfully as I could. "But I am very thankful for the prayers, and I do ask that you continue to pray for me." They were disappointed, but thankfully they accepted what I had said and moved on to the next person.

While their service was different to me and something that I would likely be comfortable doing on a regular basis, I respected their beliefs, their hope, and their faith. I learned some things about my friend and her congregation that I didn't know before because of the open mind I had from the beginning, and I feel like I am a wiser person today for the knowledge I gained.

*****

I mentioned that my friend Kelly had also been a victim of the shooting. We were both in the prayer circle. We were both shot (fortunately, the bullet that hit her only grazed her back, but it was enough to leave a lifelong mark—a daily physical reminder to her of what Michael did). We both saw some pretty gruesome things. But what Kelly witnessed was, in my opinion, much worse than what I saw. She saw Michael firing the gun. She saw students frantically trying to dodge bullets. And, worst of all, after Kayce had been shot and left unconscious, it was Kelly who identified Kayce for the paramedics. Kelly's two best friends were Kayce and me. Imagine seeing both of your best friends shot and having to identify one of them in a situation like that. Kelly struggled for years with those images in her mind and had to seek professional help. And, don't forget, she was just fifteen years old when this happened.

The day of the shooting, I forgave Michael for what he had done (I will talk more about how and why I did that in the chapter on forgiveness). Kelly, on the other hand—a God-fearing, Christian woman who is one of the nicest and most caring people I have ever known—did not forgive him and still hasn't to this day. At his sentencing, she said to him "I would love to see you get the death penalty" and "I hope you're suffering as much as we are"—words that many of us might want to say to a murderer. Her stance since then has softened a bit, and I think she has opened her mind to the possibility of one day forgiving him, which I find extremely admirable. She may still be years away from being able to do it, if at all, but just leaving open that possibility is where it has to begin.

Despite our differences in that regard, Kelly has been empathetic toward me for forgiving Michael. Because one of her best friends, Kayce, died in the shooting, I wouldn't have been surprised if Kelly had been upset with me for forgiving him, especially as quickly as I did, but she never has been. Just as I have always been empathetic toward her feelings, she has been the same way toward mine. She knows that what we experienced during the shooting was different, that there were differences in how we were raised that may have influenced our feelings afterward, and that being best friends doesn't mean we have to agree with each other about everything. She has taken the time to learn and understand my position, and I hers. We were best friends before the shooting and remain best friends today despite the different effects the shooting had on us.

I even tried to empathize with Michael when I found out he was appealing his case years later in an attempt to be released from prison and transferred to a psychiatric hospital. I don't think he should ever be let out of prison, but my attempt to empathize with him enabled me to learn a lot about the process he was following and what his future possibilities were.

You see, some people who are sentenced to prison can seek to be transferred to a psychiatric hospital in order to get the medical care they feel they need. Once that hospital and the courts deem them to no longer be a threat, they can be released into society. It's similar to the case of John Hinckley, Jr. If you are not familiar with him, he attempted to assassinate President Ronald Reagan in 1981. Because Hinckley was found guilty by reason of insanity, he never went to prison; he went to a psychiatric institution instead. As his mental health improved, he was allowed overnight visits at his parents' house. Those visits became more frequent over the years, and he was eventually released to his mother's care for good in 2016 despite the objections of some who felt he could still be a threat to others.

Michael pleaded "guilty, but mentally ill," which is not the same as Hinckley's plea of guilty by reason of insanity. With his plea, Michael was sentenced to prison and not a hospital (though he would still receive medical treatment in prison). However, his attorneys and family have been trying for years since then to get him transferred to a hospital. They have argued that he would receive better care there, but they also know that once he is in a hospital, he will have a better chance of one day being released.

When I heard what Michael was trying to do, I tried to empathize with him and educated myself about his situation. All of that stuff about Hinckley that I just mentioned—the only reason I know all of that is because of my research on Michael's situation. And so I asked myself:

Would Michael be better off in a hospital?

Is it possible that being in prison is making his mental state worse?

Would he still really be a threat to society after all these years if he were one day released?

Can an argument be made that his family, which lost their son and brother when he was just fourteen years old, deserves a second chance with him?

It was after my two-hour face-to-face visit in prison with Michael in 2007 that I found my answers.

I was told by his attorneys before our visit that he was in a very fragile mental state. They said he would likely need to take several breaks during our meeting, and that there was a pretty good chance he wouldn't even make it through the full two hours. I could tell when he and I first came face to face that day that something wasn't right about him—he continually looked down at the floor and swung one of his arms back and forth, which I was later told were side effects of the medication he had taken. But in terms of his mental health during that meeting, the medication was working perfectly. He easily made it through the two hours, didn't have to take a single break, and our conversation was as normal as could be.

When we left the prison, I told Mandy that I saw no reason why he should be transferred to a hospital. She completely agreed. It was obvious during the course of our conversation that he was getting the treatment he needed in prison. And, let's remember, he was in prison for a reason— he killed three girls and injured five other students. Those he murdered have no appeals, and there must be consequences for his actions. Many would argue that even if he weren't getting proper treatment in prison, he should still be locked up. What might happen if he were to be moved to a hospital, eventually freed, and then decided to stop taking his medication at home? Is there a chance he could hurt someone again? I think it would always be a possibility, one that the Paducah community should never have to worry about.

Empathy requires tolerance, but it does not require that you agree.

*****

On a much lighter note, but still with regard to empathy, you would not believe how many times in the more than two decades I have been in a wheelchair, as I am wheeling myself down a hallway, someone has jokingly said to me, "Hey, watch the speed limit!" And they laugh...and they laugh...and they laugh. I know, it's not that funny. But they think it is. And with a forced smile I respond with, "There's no speed limit in the hallway." And they laugh some more. And then they say it again the next time they pass me, making it even less funny to me than the first time.

Yes, it's such a harmless and silly thing to be bothered by. Believe me, I know that. But we all have our pet peeves, those little things people say or do that bug us for whatever reason. I don't know what it is about the speed limit comment that gets to me. Maybe it's that I hear it so often. Or maybe it's a reminder to me that they don't have to worry about a "speed limit" because they can use their legs to walk. Or maybe it's just that nobody has come up with something more creative, like "You should install a horn on that thing!" or "Don't forget to use your turn signal!" Okay, those comments aren't very funny either, but at least they're different.

The point I want to make is that while it's still irritating when someone makes the speed limit comment to me, I don't get as annoyed about it as I once did because I have learned to see their perspective. The reason they are likely saying it is simply to break the ice and to relate to me in some way. Believe it or not, even in today's world, seeing a young person in a wheelchair makes many people uncomfortable because they don't know what to say or how to act. Of course, they shouldn't speak or behave any differently than if I were walking past them. But when some people encounter a situation they aren't used to, they often feel they need to address it in some way to make themselves feel more comfortable. Being in a wheelchair is my normal, but it's not normal to them. And with that understanding of their view, I am able to be less annoyed by what they say or do in relation to it.

Here is another interesting example that involves my wheelchair.

For those who don't know, a person paralyzed from the chest down can still drive a car. I got my license soon after my initial rehabilitation. I control the car using a hand gear that is attached with a rod to the gas and brake pedals. I guess it's similar to controlling a motorcycle. It's easy to do, especially compared to getting into my car, which is quite difficult. To do that, I have to open the door, move my wheelchair as close to the car as I can, put a plastic board between my chair and the car seat, use my arms to push myself from the chair onto the board, and slide my butt across it until I'm in the car. Then I have to reach over and take my wheelchair apart— each wheel has to come off and the seat has to fold down— and toss it all in the back seat. When I get out of the car, I do the same things, but in reverse. Yes, it is as exhausting as it sounds and it takes time, but having gotten a rhythm down, it's really not that difficult…unless someone tries to help me.

Sometimes, when I am in a parking lot and about to get into my car, people will ask if they can assist me with my wheelchair. Unless I am struggling because the weather is bad or because I am not feeling well, I will politely turn down their offer. As many people with disabilities or debilitating illnesses will tell you, we always greatly appreciate offers to help, but when we say no, we really mean no, and for good reason. In the case of me getting into my car, even when I say no, people will just go ahead and try to help. They will attempt to take my chair apart, which isn't easy to do if they have never done it. So I have to show them how, which takes more time than just doing it myself. This becomes even more aggravating if I am in a rush to pick up my kids or get to an appointment. Then I have to ask them to put it in the backseat, but sometimes they set it out of my reach from the front seat so that when I get to my next destination, I can't get out of the car on my own. If they had only listened to me when I had said no…

What I do when they don't listen is take a deep breath and focus on putting myself in their shoes. They aren't trying to aggravate me—they are actually trying to do the exact opposite and help me. They may be thinking, "She is telling me no because she doesn't want to inconvenience me, but she's not inconveniencing me, so I'll just go ahead and help her." Or they may be on a mission to do a good deed for someone and I am their chosen one that day, so nothing is going to stop them. As much as I might want to scream, "Get away! Don't touch my chair!" I would never be that rude—

because I can see their perspective. Plus, if I were to insist that they leave me alone, what would they do if they were ever in that situation again with a person who really did need their help? Would they just look the other way, too afraid to offer? I don't want their meeting with me to be the reason they stop helping other people. Yes, they may have created a hassle for me, but by empathizing, it makes their "help" a little easier to accept.

Something else I often encounter is that when I am in a crowded place and approaching a mom with a young child, she will swoop up that child as if she were rescuing her from being hit by a car that is going sixty miles an hour down a neighborhood street. This happens more often than you might think, especially in malls or at summer festivals. It's very dramatic, and actually quite comical now that I understand their view of it. What I want to say as I pass by the mom gripping her kid in her arms as if she just saved her life is, "Honey, I may not be able to walk, but I can still see. I'm really not going to run over your kid." I mean, seriously, it's a manual wheelchair that I might get up to speeds of two miles per hour (see, I *do* watch the speed limit). I am in control of it. I'm not out trying to set a speed record, tallying how many kids I can mow down in the process.

Some people in wheelchairs might be offended by the mom's over-the-top reaction, but her perspective may be that she's more worried about her kid not paying attention and aimlessly walking into my path without looking, or she just wants to make sure I have enough space to pass without her kid being a hindrance. As I will talk about in the chapter on laughter, there are some things you just need to laugh at, and this is one I am able to laugh at now because I can empathize with her.

*****

When my oldest son, Logan, was nine years old, he had a meltdown one day when he got home from school because he had forgotten his dollar to get ice cream at lunch. That may seem like no big deal to an adult, or even to a young teenager, but it can be a major catastrophe to a kid his age. Having ice cream was a huge treat and event at his school each week. Because he forgot his money, he was the only kid in his class who didn't get it that day, which made him feel left out and even resulted in some kids teasing him about it.

A little empathy from both Logan and me went a long way toward helping him through this situation.

The empathy from me was realizing that even though Logan and I have the same DNA and live under the same roof, we do, in some respects, live in different worlds. I knew that missing out on ice cream was not a big deal in the big picture of life, but he was too young to be able to figure that out on his own. I didn't empathize with him by babying him or running to the store to get him his own ice cream, but I didn't dismiss his feelings, either—in the daily world of a nine-year-old, there can be "serious" social ramifications to being the only one not participating in something. What I did do was use it as a chance to teach him about responsibility ("Don't forget your money next time") and how to keep a situation in perspective. And by learning to keep it in perspective, he was able to empathize himself. I helped him realize that while he didn't get ice cream that day, there were nine-year-olds in our very own country who were homeless right at that moment and didn't get food of any kind that day. Suddenly, not getting ice cream didn't seem so awful to him.

I think parents and their kids often butt heads because of their failure to try to put themselves in the other's world. We all face some sort of stress each day, which can be at different levels depending on our age, upbringing, socioeconomic status, opportunities or non-opportunities, relationships with others, responsibilities, etc. And we have every right to feel the way we feel. But the more we try to empathize, the more understanding and peace we can bring not only to each other, but to our own lives.

Fortunately, the teasing Logan endured from other students for not being able to get ice cream was short-lived and forgotten about the next day. But we all know that simple teasing can often lead to bullying, which can create a host of other problems for those being bullied—lost sleep, social anxiety, eating disorders, a drop in grades, general misbehavior, the desire to seek revenge against the bully, thoughts of hurting oneself to escape the bullying.

If a bully could truly see and understand the perspective of the person he is bullying and empathize with him, might that cause him to change his ways? Maybe not always, but I believe in many cases, yes.

A friend of mine told me a story of when his family moved to another state when he was a kid and he had to attend a new middle school. It was a very difficult transition for him, and it was made even more difficult by one mean person. His very first day of school, that mean person approached him at his locker and asked him if his parents had insurance on him. "Uh, I don't know," he said, wondering where such an odd question was going to lead.

"Well, they better," the bully said, "because if you don't give me a pencil right now, I'm going to beat the crap out of you."

Imagine that. A brand new school, few friends, miles away from what had always been your home, and this is how you are greeted on your very first day. I tell you to imagine it, but I know that, sadly, many of you may have experienced or are experiencing something similar.

He gave the bully the pencil since the last thing he wanted to do was get into a fight, especially on his first day. The next day the bully did the same thing again, and my friend gave up another pencil. On the third day, they were in the cafeteria for lunch when the bully walked by my friend's table. Other kids at the table started picking on the bully because someone at the table had found out the bully's real first name, which was a very unusual name. As much as my friend was tempted to become a bully himself and join in on the razzing, he didn't. Instead, he kept a straight face as he and the bully locked eyes.

"I know it sounds weird at that age, but I felt like the two of us made a serious connection at that moment," my friend said. "Like he now knew what my perspective was when he had bullied me. I figured the next day, as a result of those kids teasing him, he would either be meaner to me or he would leave me alone for good.

"He left me alone for good."

What's fascinating about that story, though not at all uncommon, is that people who are bullied never forget. That incident happened more than thirty years ago. I bet if that bully were asked about the threats he made over pencils, he wouldn't remember it. It was just another ordinary day in his life. But my friend recalls every detail—who said what, where they were standing when it happened, even what month and year it happened. That bully might have possibly become a better person in later years, but my friend's recollection of him is that he was a bully.

*****

One way I challenge the students I work with who are bullies is to ask them how they want to be remembered in life. Whether you treat people in a good way or bad way, they will always remember how you made them feel. If you treat others well, they will remember it. If you make them feel horrible, they will remember that, too, even decades later, because of the agony you inflicted upon them. If you are a bully today, ask yourself if that's what you want your legacy to be, because that *is* what it will be to those you hurt.

Let's look at it from a different perspective:

Think about your life twenty years from now. Assume you are married with children, a good job, and new friends who know little or nothing about your childhood. One day, while at the store with your wife and kids, you run into a guy you used to bully all the time. It is the first thing that comes to your mind and to his mind, and you both feel uncomfortable about it. Since you are older and wiser, you greet him kindly and assume that the past is the past. But he still has the emotional scars of what you did, and he has since gained the confidence to let you know it.

And he does.

In front of your wife and kids, the people who love you and look up to you, he calls you out for what you did to him. He even gets visibly emotional about it. How would you feel? How would you feel about your kids, who see you as their hero, hearing this man say that their dad was an awful person who made his life miserable for absolutely no reason? Embarrassed and ashamed, I presume. And how would you explain that to your family? Saying, "But that was so long ago; we were just kids and I was just teasing," won't carry much weight when the guy you bullied still has the scars all these years later.

Take charge of your legacy right now. Seek to empathize with everyone you encounter, whether it's a simple conversation on social media or someone you meet at school. Consider these four steps toward empathy that I share with my students:

1.) Don't judge the person.
2.) Listen to the person.
3.) Put yourself in that person's shoes.
4.) Now ask yourself how you feel about that person.

Author Marvin J. Ashton said: "If we could look into each other's hearts and understand the unique challenges each of us faces, I think we would treat each other much more gently, with more love, patience, tolerance, and care."

And do you know what the best part is about that statement? Every one of us can do it simply by deciding that we want to.

Take Action!
Empathize

❦

Activity #1: There is a two-and-a-half minute entertaining Sesame Street video starring actor Mark Ruffalo and Sesame Street character Murray. Before doing the next activity or any other activity on empathy, watch this humorous clip to get engaged in the topic:

Watch it at https://youtu.be/9_1Rt1R4xbM

Activity #2: A classic example of the power of empathy is the book *Alexander and the Terrible, Horrible, No Good, Very Bad Day.* If you have not read it (or seen the movie), take the time to read this short story. After you have read it, do a role playing exercise. Have someone be Alexander and a few other students serve as a panel of interviewers who question Alexander about his day. Have each interviewer provide some expression of empathy as Alexander shares what his day has been like.

Activity #3: In a small group, each person should generate five ideas of things that cause them to have a terrible, horrible, no good, very bad day. Write each idea on a Post-it. Put all of the Post-its on a larger piece of paper. Work as a group to identify as many empathetic responses as possible for each one. Keep in mind that words, body language, and actions can be used to express empathy.

Activity #4: Pair with another person. Person A should think of a story to tell that has some detail to it, such as a vacation experience or something else fun he or she did over the summer. Person A should start the story with a simple sentence, such as "We went on vacation this summer to Florida." It is Person B's job to keep the story flowing with empathetic listening by asking open-ended questions to what Person A says, such as "What did you do when you were in Florida?" Questions don't have to necessarily be asked after every single statement; only when the opportunity presents itself. When finished, discuss how well Person B listened and asked questions, and if he or she can now empathize with everything Person A described.

Journal Entry: When did you most recently experience empathy from someone? When have you expressed empathy toward another? How does acknowledging understanding of another's unfortunate events improve relationships?

Forgive

"When deep injury is done to us, we never recover until we forgive…Forgiveness does not change the past, but it does enlarge the future."
–Mary Karen Read, victim of the 2007 shooting at Virginia Tech University

THE DAY OF THE Heath shooting, while I was in the hospital and knowing that I would likely never walk again, I told my mom something that I expected would shock her, but my heart told me to say it to her anyway.

"Mama," I said. "I want you to know that I forgive Michael for what he did to me."

I was right. It did shock her. But only for a brief moment. She wasn't shocked because she didn't think I should or could forgive him. I think it was more that the shooting had just happened hours earlier, I was only fifteen years old, and I was in the midst of a very traumatic situation.

"God bless you, honey," she said as she stroked my hair. "I guess if you can forgive him, then so can I."

Two questions I usually receive from students and adults are, "Why did you forgive him?" and "How were you able to forgive him?" The answers, I believe, are intertwined.

Less than two years before the shooting, when I was in eighth grade, I was baptized into my church. So, yes, I do rely on my faith a lot, and I do credit my faith for helping me forgive Michael. But I know not everyone believes in a higher power. Does that mean they aren't as likely to choose to forgive as someone who does believe, or that it's more difficult for them to forgive? Some believers may think so, but I don't. We all have the same capacity to forgive because forgiveness is primarily about self-healing, not about the person being forgiven.

The reason I forgave Michael had little to do with him and everything to do with me. I forgave him for my own emotional well-being. If it made him feel better, too, then that was a bonus.

If I still hadn't forgiven him today, I shudder to think of what my life would be like. I don't see how I would have had the mental fortitude to live in a meaningful way. Being angry is exhausting. As trite as that sounds, anger can take a lot out of us emotionally, which can also affect our physical health and mental stability. I'm not sure that I'd even be married or have kids, or that I'd be able to tell my story or work with the students I work with.

If someone does something wrong to you, why let that person's actions continue to haunt you and mess with your life each day? I know, easier said than done. But it *can* be done. Author Jonathan Lockwood Huie said: "Forgiving is not a gift to someone else. Forgiving is your gift to yourself— a great gift—the gift of happiness."

Think about that. Forgiveness is a gift to yourself. How profound.

I realize that some people or actions are not so easy to forgive. If someone killed my child, I am not sure how I would be able to forgive that person. I could see myself feeling an overwhelming amount of anger for a very long time, maybe forever, if I were the parent of Nicole, Kayce, or Jessica. Or, if that bullet that had scraped the back of Mandy's neck had been an inch to the left and killed her, would I have forgiven Michael? I don't know how I could have. But my hope would be that, with time, while I would never fully recover from the loss of my child or my sister, I would be able to at least forgive enough to live my life with purpose.

*****

One process to follow when you want to forgive someone is to take the person you want to forgive out of the scenario. Look strictly at how you were wronged and ask yourself, "How does this make me feel?" "How is it affecting my daily activities?" and "Is this how I want to live and feel for the rest of my life?" Focus not on the person, but on the effects that person's actions have had on you. Because it's not about fixing that person—it's about fixing you.

For example, let's say your parent is driving you to school and another driver crashes into you. The other driver and your parent walk away unscathed, but the damage to your body is so severe that you end up in a hospital and rehab for months. It has completely turned your life upside down. You miss a lot of school. Your sports or dance season is over. You can't be in the school play. This all could and should cause you to be angry at the driver who hit you. Very angry. But *staying* angry at him as he continues to live his life does not help you at all, and it is certainly not affecting him since that anger is inside your own mind.

So, let's remove him from the equation and ask those three questions.

How does being in a hospital with broken bones and being out of commission for a lengthy amount of time make you feel? It infuriates you. You have never experienced anything like this before, and you wouldn't wish it upon your worst enemy.

How is it affecting your life? It's caused you a lot of physical and emotional pain. Your team won the big game last night and you couldn't play. Student council elections are coming up, but you can't run for office because you can't be there. The talent show is in a couple weeks, but you can't perform because of your injuries.

And now the big question: Is this how you want to live and feel for the rest of your life—with this anger and resentment hanging over you? Of course not! As angry as you are, and as much right as you have to be angry, it's a horrible way to continue going through life. You want to be happy again. You want to emotionally and physically feel good again.

These answers lead us to a fourth question, and a very important one: so what are you going to do about it?

And that's where the actual act of forgiving really kicks in.

Because what you are going to do about it is work your tail off to get back to full strength and get back the life that you had before (or as close to it as you can) and do the things that you want to do to make yourself happy again. Not one bit of the focus will be on the person who did this to you; it will be squarely on you. And when it's on you, the person who wronged you will fade from your mind. Not completely. Not forever. But enough for you to focus on and live the life you want to live. Even if you haven't formally forgiven him, you have at least forgotten about him enough that you have taken back your life, which is what you set out to do—and had great difficulty doing when he was the focus instead of you.

When I did my rehab, Michael was so far from my mind that I didn't even know what was happening to him. From the day he shot us until his sentencing a year later, he sat in a jail cell—but I can't say that I really even knew that. I assumed it, I guess. I knew he wasn't at home. But I didn't know what jail he was in, what his days were like, or what he was doing about his case. I was focused on getting myself better so that I could go to school again. I was focused on learning how to live my new life in a wheelchair.

Sure, it was difficult to not think of him each day when I knew he was the reason I was in the situation I was in, but he would appear as just a blip in my mind and then be gone. At no time did I think of him beyond that. Even a few weeks after the shooting, when I finally had an emotional breakdown at the hospital and cried buckets of tears for the first time, I wasn't thinking about him or asking why he had done what he had done. I was crying because I was worried about myself and how I was going to reclaim my life. If I hadn't forgiven him, I don't think I would have been able to rehabilitate myself as quickly as I did.

71

Focus on the issue at hand, not on the person who caused the issue at hand. The sooner you can forgive, the easier that will be to do.

*****

When I was in eighth grade, Kelly had been dating this kid in our class. They had been going out for only about a week and, from my viewpoint, they weren't very serious. That was confirmed in my mind when I had run into him at a couple of places and he flirted with me. After that week, he broke up with Kelly and asked me out. I said yes, not thinking she would care. But, oh, was I wrong. I obviously hadn't done a very good job putting myself in her shoes, because she cared a lot. She was furious that her best friend would "betray" her. I explained to her that I never would have agreed to go out with him if I had known it would bother her. It took some time, but eventually she forgave me.

While she was too young to know the steps I just went through in the previous example, Kelly essentially asked herself those questions in her effort to forgive me.

How did me dating that guy make her feel? It made her very angry.

How was it affecting her life? She was losing sleep over it because her best friend was dating her ex-boyfriend. It was understandable that it upset her.

Is that how she wanted to feel? No, not at all.

So what was she going to do about it? She eventually realized that losing a guy she had dated for one week was not worth losing a best friend over. She removed him from the equation and focused on what she ultimately wanted: to heal our friendship. We talked it out one day, she forgave me, and we saved our relationship. Also, I broke up with him, because no guy in eighth grade is worth more than your best friend.

*****

In a more recent case, a friend told me that his neighbor got upset with him about something. I don't want to disclose much about it because I want to protect the privacy of both, but it was really a minor issue between two neighbors that could have easily been discussed in a calm manner and worked out in a mature way in a matter of minutes, but his neighbor instead lost her cool. She screamed and cursed and even threatened to hurt my friend, leaving him in complete shock that she would treat him that way, especially given that they had never once had an issue before.

My friend said that he feels she owes him an apology; at the very least he would like an explanation for the outburst. But no matter what happens, even if it's nothing, he has already forgiven her. Why? Because they have to live by each other and he doesn't want to go outside each day feeling any anger or resentment toward her. What happened between them made him feel bad; he didn't like that he and a neighbor weren't getting along. So he removed her from the equation and determined that in order to be able to walk outside his house each day and tolerate seeing her, he would need to forgive her. He didn't do it for her, but for himself. They still don't speak to each other, but because he has forgiven her, he hardly thinks about her anymore and isn't bothered by her presence.

The funny thing is that the neighbor's beef with him was so irrational that she may not care less that she has been forgiven, and she probably doesn't even think she needs to be forgiven. She would probably try to justify her outburst if asked about it. But, again, he didn't forgive her for her. He did it for himself, for his own psychological health. His hope is that his neighbor comes around one day and apologizes. If she doesn't, he is still in a good place mentally.

*****

When I was in elementary and middle school, I had some issues with my weight. So during the summer before entering seventh grade at Heath Middle School, I decided to do something about it. I exercised. I ate well. I weighed myself daily. By the time school had started, I had dropped from a size sixteen to a size five. It was an incredible transformation in such a short time. I was very proud of what I had done.

But that pride vanished the first day of school when a girl asked me if I was anorexic. She was with some friends, who laughed at me after she asked. I had been made fun of for years for being too heavy, and now I was being made fun of for being too thin? And her friends piled on with their laughter? I told her I wasn't anorexic, dropped my head, and went over to my desk to sit down. I was devastated.

To put it bluntly, they made me feel like crap. Their words stung. They made me second guess myself about all of the hard work I had put in that summer to lose the weight, and I hated that they made me feel that way. But what I did about it was remove them from the situation so that I could better see that, yes, losing the weight was a good thing, and I wasn't going to let a bunch of jealous girls who were never my friends to begin with bring me down.

It took me a while, but I forgave her and her friends. It doesn't mean I tried to become their friend—quite frankly, I wanted nothing to do with them. Nor did I tell them I forgave them since they were nothing but bullies and wouldn't have cared anyway, but I forgave them in my mind and heart so that I could concentrate on school and on keeping my weight down. I focused on the many positive comments several other people had given me about my new look, and I never let anything those girls said bother me again.

*****

In the summer of 2012, there was a shooting in a movie theatre in Aurora, Colorado. Twelve people were killed and dozens more were injured. One of the victims, Pierce O'Farrill, was shot three times. During his recovery, he spoke to the media and said that he had forgiven the shooter. It was very similar to what I had done with Michael. And the public reaction was also similar. People wanted to know how he was able to do it.

"Of course, I forgive him with all my heart," Mr. O'Farrill was quoted as saying. "When I saw him in his hearing, I felt nothing but sorrow for him—he's just a lost soul right now. I want to see him sometime. The first thing I want to say to him is 'I forgive you'…"

I think calling the shooter a "lost soul" was very telling about the type of person Mr. O'Farrill is, which contributed to his ability to forgive. Many people called the shooter evil, Satan, scum, and just about any other negative or derogatory term you can think of, and I would agree that those feelings were justified. But Mr. O'Farrill was obviously able to find a way to empathize with the shooter. He did not agree with his actions or vindicate him at all, but he was able to empathize enough that he could forgive him and focus on his own recovery.

There are some who will say that if Mr. O'Farrill can forgive in a case such as that, or if I can forgive Michael after what he did, then everybody should be able to forgive anyone for just about anything. But I disagree. Do not compare your situation to another. We have established that every one of us is different and has a unique story, which will make our approaches to situations such as this very different. If by me forgiving Michael you are inspired to forgive somebody, then that's absolutely wonderful! But do not forgive someone just because someone says you should. Work at it the best you can, but do it on your terms, when you are ready.

*****

Here is a story in which, despite a lack of listening and a lack of empathy, forgiveness still prevailed.

In 2012, I was a guest on the old daytime talk show *Anderson Live*. It was hosted by Anderson Cooper, a journalist for CNN. He asked me to be on the show to address "murderabilia." Murderabilia is a combination of the words "murder" and "memorabilia." It refers to items such as autographed photos and handwritten letters that people obtain through the mail from notorious killers and then sell online for profit.

It really is as sick as it sounds, and yes, there are some Michael Carneal items out there.

The people who do this obviously don't know how or don't care to empathize with the families of the victims. They will try to pass these items off as "historical," but they're not. When you write letters to the killers, ask them to send an autograph or piece of artwork, and then turn around and sell it and pocket the money, there is nothing historical about it. In essence, they are simply profiting from someone's murder.

When I appeared on the show, it was with a couple of guys who run these businesses. While hesitant to be in the same studio with them, I went on hoping that seeing me in a wheelchair and hearing my story would make them think twice about what they were doing.

It didn't.

I said what I wanted to say. Other victims on the show said what they wanted to say. Anderson was clearly in our corner and gave these guys a piece of his mind. But they didn't listen at all. They heard a bunch of words, but they didn't listen. They couldn't have cared less about what we had to say.

When I left the studio and was on a plane home later that day, I was upset, as you might imagine. I was upset that they didn't listen to us. I was upset that they didn't try to put themselves in my shoes or in the shoes of any of the victims' families. I was upset that they were also on their way home probably discussing who the next murderer was they were going to go after for autographs.

But by the time my plane had landed, I had forgiven them.

Why?

Because I knew my kids and my husband were going to be waiting for me at home, excited to have their mom and wife back, and because I knew that any more energy I expended on those guys was not going to do me any good whatsoever.

How was I able to forgive them? By believing in the basic goodness of people to not purchase this stuff from them. Yes, there would be some out there who would buy a signature of a killer because they think it's cool, but I think most of humanity knows how horrible and flat out wrong it is to get involved in something like this. I wish the sellers would stop, especially out of respect for the families of Nicole, Kayce, and Jessica. But they have free will to do it, just as I had free will on that plane ride home to forgive them and move forward.

*****

Something else in relation to forgiveness that you could be confronted with one day, or maybe have been already, is what to do when someone comes to you seeking your forgiveness. In this case, it could become more about that person than about you, which can create a very uncomfortable situation if you're not ready to forgive.

My advice is that if you're not ready to forgive, don't do it. Don't be phony and force something that is not there. It is still about you first. But hopefully you will at least be able to appreciate that if someone did something to hurt you and is asking you to forgive them, your relationship means something to them and/or they are genuinely remorseful. I would recommend you at least thank them for approaching you and ask them to give you some time to sort things out in your mind. Hopefully, whatever they did to you is something you will be able to forgive in the near future, especially since they are asking. If not, maybe the two of you can at least continue the dialogue, which is a good start toward healing.

Yes, I know there are some con artists out there who might manipulate you, get caught, say they're sorry, and seek your forgiveness so that they can take advantage of you again. Always forgive when you feel you are ready, but don't be so gullible as to repeat getting burned. Let's say you invite a new friend over to your house and he steals money from your bedroom. Even if he gets caught, says he will never do it again, asks for your forgiveness, and you decide to forgive him, you may not want to invite him up to your room right away with money laying around. Yes, you have to have trust in every true friendship, but there is nothing wrong with easing your way back into it and rebuilding that trust over time.

When the request for forgiveness is genuine, though, it can begin to remove a lot of pain for both of you, and it can make it much easier for you to forgive considering the person's vulnerability. I know I had to open my heart after the shooting to a few people who felt guilty for what Michael had done.

One was a friend who claimed that Michael had told him in advance of the shooting that "something big" was going to happen at school. If you hear a kid say that today, you have to take it seriously given all of the violence in schools the past two decades. But back then, school violence was very rare. Few people ever heard threats like that, and if they did, they weren't taken seriously. But this friend was sick to his stomach after the shooting—not just that day or for weeks after, but for years. He called me crying when we were in college, telling me how guilty he still felt. I didn't feel like he needed to be forgiven—I didn't blame him in the least for what Michael had done—but I made it clear to him that if forgiveness was what he wanted from me, then it was his. I didn't want him persecuting himself anymore. He was a good person who deserved to live free of any guilt.

Another case involved a kid Michael specifically named during his interrogation as someone who had bullied him. Michael didn't blame the shooting completely on the bullying, but he did say at the time and when I had met with him in prison that it was likely a factor. When that boy learned that Michael had called him out while being questioned by authorities, he felt horrible.

He came to me soon after the shooting and asked me to forgive him for what he had done. This wasn't quite as open and shut as forgiving my other friend I just mentioned, but it was still easy to forgive this person. The fact that he felt guilty and sought my forgiveness showed me how much his bullying of Michael had weighed on him. He needed my forgiveness to forgive himself. If he had been the only one responsible for what Michael had done (for example, if he had given Michael the guns and encouraged him to shoot people), this would have been more difficult.

I can't say how I would have reacted to his request in that case. But, given the situation, what good would it have done either of us if I couldn't forgive him? Forgiving him helped him move forward with his life, which I'm sure positively affected many others close to him. For me, it was another burden lifted.

*****

A couple more brief points about forgiveness.

You have probably figured out this first one, but I want to make it very clear: forgiving someone does not absolve the person who committed the wrong-doing.

Telling Michael I forgave him did not mean that I didn't think he should go to prison. Too often people associate forgiveness with exoneration of the person being forgiven, and that's wrong. The only one being exonerated is you...from having to carry the weight of what that person did to you. When Michael pleaded guilty, I was there to make sure the judge knew what he had done to me so that he would receive the proper sentence. Each time he has appealed his case, I have been there in court to argue against it. When he is eligible for parole, I will be there to try to keep him behind bars for the safety of our community. And I have done or will do all of that despite having forgiven him. There are consequences for actions; forgiveness doesn't eliminate those consequences.

The second point is that, despite what some "tough guys" may say or think, forgiveness is not a sign of weakness. In fact, it is the complete opposite. It is a sign of incredible strength. Anybody can stay angry at someone when they've been wronged. That's easy to do. But to be able to show mercy to someone who has hurt you in some way is courageous and powerful and to be admired. Don't ever doubt that.

If you are having a difficult time forgiving someone, it's okay. Just try not to slam the door shut on the possibility of it one day happening, even if it's years from now. Like all of the other principles, forgiveness is a piece of the puzzle toward lasting love and peace within your life and the lives of those around you. Harboring anger or resentment toward someone can be understandable in many situations, but the longer you hold on to it, the more potential it has to define who you are, and the more difficult it will be for you and those close to you to live the lives you want and deserve.

Forgiveness may or may not emotionally free the person who wronged you, but it will definitely free you.

Take Action!
Forgive

૪ુ

Activity #1: "Holding onto anger is like drinking poison and expecting the other person to die." That quote (some have attributed it to Buddha, others say the author is unknown...in either case, it is a great quote) is one of many found on the Internet that relate to forgiveness. In a small group, see how many quotes you can find that describe forgiveness and its benefits. Which ones resonate the most with you? Write the quotes in your journal.

Activity #2: In that same small group, work together to come up with seven words to create the acronym "FORGIVE." In other words, what word can you think of that begins with the letter "F" that relates to forgiveness? And then the letter "O." And so on. Be creative by trying to come up with words that the other groups may not think of.

F
O
R
G
I
V
E

Activity #3: One of the gravest atrocities in the history of the world was the Holocaust, yet many Holocaust survivors have forgiven the Germans. Using the Internet, see how many Holocaust survivors you can find (through articles and videos) who have found a way to forgive. Read or listen to their stories to learn why they forgave, how long it took them, and how they were able to do it.

Activity #4: In a small group, discuss some hypothetical situations in which you may have to seek someone's forgiveness. Maybe you embarrassed someone in front of other people or talked about someone behind their back or didn't follow through with helping someone like you said you would. Once these situations have been identified, discuss what actions you could take above and beyond saying "I'm sorry" to make amends with the person from whom you are seeking forgiveness.

Journal Entry: Think about someone who has recently done something to hurt you and whom you have not forgiven. How did that person's transgression hurt you at the time, and how does it continue to affect your life today? If you were to forgive that person today, would a weight be lifted off your shoulders? How would it improve your life? How would you feel if that person asked you for forgiveness? Would you be able to forgive? If not, is there something else that person could do to be forgiven? If you are not ready to forgive, can you at least keep the door open to that possibility in the future?

Laugh…a Lot

"Always laugh when you can. It is cheap medicine."
– Lord Byron

FINDING HUMOR IN CIRCUMSTANCES that trigger negative or stress-related emotions is difficult. Whether it's something as serious as a school shooting or as minor as someone cutting in front of you in line at the amusement park, it's not a natural laughing matter. Why would you even consider cracking a smile? But, at the appropriate time, laughter can be just the remedy you need for the benefit of your mental health and overall well-being. It can diffuse a tense situation, save a relationship, or simply soften an uncomfortable moment. Sometimes the opportunity to laugh will emerge on its own. Other times you will have to make an effort to harness it. Whatever the case, don't ever discount its value.

When I returned to Heath several months after the shooting, some of us created a support group to talk about all that we had experienced. We met a couple times a week, and anybody was welcome. One of the girls who participated who had always had a knack for making me laugh brought that humor to what otherwise would have been a pretty depressing group. Laughter was how she dealt with most of her problems, and she helped me and others understand that no matter how awful a situation was, it was okay to laugh. There was no disrespect intended or shown toward me or any of the other shooting victims—humor was just one way we dealt with something so heavy, and I have continued to utilize it as a coping mechanism ever since.

During my first year at Murray State, I often returned to Paducah on weekends. It was only about forty-five minutes away and I still had a lot of close friends there, including one of my best friends, Taylor, who was a year younger than me and a senior at Heath (she was the one I rode to school with the morning of the shooting). One Saturday night at home during the winter, long before Netflix and other streaming media existed, Taylor and I wanted to drive to the video store to rent a movie. Because it was snowing, our parents said we shouldn't go. But being in college—I was an adult teenager now and knew *everything*, right?—and even though I had never driven in snow, I decided I could handle it. So, off we went.

I chose what I expected would be the best and safest route to the store, a road that I figured not many people would use in that weather. It was a two-lane country highway with storm ditches on either side. Paducah had a lot of roads like that; there weren't many options to get from Point A to Point B. It turned out on that night, I was correct about the scarcity of drivers using that road…but it only takes one to create a problem.

The snow was lightly falling when we left the house and it was extremely cold, so the roads were slick. Snow plows and salt trucks hadn't been out yet. Being a rookie driver in such weather, I was going about as slowly as I could without actually stopping the car. I was nervous, but I stayed in my lane and was doing fine. I considered turning around since the snow was getting heavier, but I figured trying to do that would be even more dangerous, so we continued on.

We had been driving for a few minutes when we saw the headlights of another car coming from the other direction, the first car other than ours that had been on that road. And wouldn't you know it, the driver was more inexperienced in bad weather than I. As we approached each other I continued at my slow and steady pace, but the other driver got nervous, hit the brake, and kept her foot on it. Bad move. Her car slid. Back and forth and back and forth her rear tires swooshed before they finally swerved around, causing her car to come at us sideways. There was no avoiding her. She was now across both lanes with a ditch on either side. I could do nothing but stop my car and wait for the wreck to happen. It's emotionally difficult when you get into a wreck. That feeling is multiplied times a hundred when you are forced to watch it slowly unfold right before your eyes and there is nothing you can do to prevent it.

The side of her car slammed into the front of mine. Her car then bounced backward, spun, and landed in the ditch. When she hit us, my airbag blasted open and the horn blared. Taylor let out piercing screams that I swear were louder than the horn. Fortunately, neither one of us was hurt. But I was worried about the other driver's condition, and that another car could come down the road and hit us.

"What do we do? What do we do? What do we do?" Taylor cried over and over.

"Calm down," I said as I fought with the airbag to get it out of my face. "We're okay. Just calm down."

"She's in the ditch!" Taylor exclaimed.

"It's okay," I assured her. I don't know why I was so calm. Maybe once you are in a school shooting, other traumatic events just don't seem that traumatic. Or maybe I just figured that one of us had to be calm, and since Taylor was already playing the freak-out card…

"Go check on her and make sure she's okay," I said to Taylor about the other driver. "If she is, come back and get me out. If not, stay with her."

"How will I get you out?" Taylor said.

"You can put my chair together or just drag me out to the ditch," I said. "I don't care how you do it. Just check on her first. If she's okay, hurry back and get me before another car comes."

As Taylor exited the car, the other driver exited hers. She climbed out of the ditch and up to the road. She physically appeared to be okay, but she was bawling.

"Are you alright?" Taylor asked her.

"I'm fine," the woman said between sobs. "But what about her?" she said pointing at me.

"She's okay," Taylor said.

"She is? Then why isn't she getting out of the car?" The woman's voice rose with concern. "Another car could hit her!"

"She can't get out on her own," Taylor said. "She's paralyzed."

The woman's face turned as white as the snow that was falling. "Oh my God!" she screamed at the top of her lungs, sobbing harder than before. Taylor didn't understand the woman's reaction until she realized what she had just said to her. The light bulb finally popped on.

"Oh gosh, no," Taylor said, spontaneously laughing. "You didn't paralyze her. She's been paralyzed for a few years."

I'm surprised she didn't knock Taylor into the next county. The woman gathered herself and exhaled a huge sigh of relief. When they came over to get me out of the car, Taylor told me what she had said that had sent the woman into a panic. I couldn't stop laughing. One nice thing about laughter is that it can be infectious, and it was exactly what we all needed at that moment. While still in a bad situation, we took advantage of being able to laugh when we could. Taylor's comment had changed our attitudes and perspectives, and it made a very traumatic event a little less traumatic. We had a couple of wrecked cars, but we were all okay and safe, which was what mattered most.

*****

The summer after the shooting, I attended the Shepherd Center's annual "Adventure Skills Workshop" in Alabama. The Shepherd Center is a hospital that cares for and rehabilitates people with catastrophic injuries, including spinal cord injuries. I would have the chance to participate in numerous strenuous outdoor activities that many paraplegics don't think they can do once they lose the use of their lower bodies. I knew it would not only challenge me physically, but it would give me an opportunity to gain some self-confidence.

My mom, dad, aunt, and uncle dropped me off at the camp with my sisters Christie and Mandy, who were allowed to attend with me. It was not unusual for campers to have siblings or friends there, mainly because most of us were not yet comfortable enough with our disabilities to be on our own.

We slept in cabins, the girls in one and the boys in another. Unlike Cardinal Hill in Lexington where the rehab was intense, this camp was much more relaxing. We got to sleep in late and participate in only those activities we wanted. I did just about everything, including water skiing, canoeing, scuba diving, tree climbing, and horseback riding. It was all very exhilarating, to say the least.

But leave it to Mandy and me to push the envelope even further with an activity that was not on our schedule—one that would result in my second brush with death in about six months.

A group of us took a break from the camp's activities for a few minutes one day and hung out near the parking lot. There was Mandy, Christie, me, a guy who was there as support for someone else, and a girl who was a paraplegic who owned a convertible. The previous week, Mandy and I had gotten our learners' permits to drive. We still hadn't driven yet, but since we were at a camp packed with adventurous activities, why not add one more to the agenda, right?

The girl with the convertible offered to let me drive it down the camp's long driveway. The car was equipped with hand controls for a paraplegic. The gas and brake controls were to the left of the steering wheel. With some rods and wires, they were connected to the gas pedal and brake, similar to the way my car is today.

Christie and Mandy helped me slide behind the wheel. The owner of the car rode in the passenger seat while Mandy sat in the back. Christie sat on the nearby grass with the guy, who had a video recorder and taped the whole thing. I admit that I was scared, but I kept the car at a slow and steady speed for the couple hundred feet I had to drive. It was nice to finally get to drive, and I made it look so easy that Mandy decided to give it a try. While it had hand controls, the car could still be driven using the actual gas pedal and brake, which is what Mandy chose to use.

I returned to my wheelchair on the grass next to Christie and the guy, and Mandy jumped in the front seat and behind the wheel. The car's owner sat next to her. Mandy went up the driveway with no problem, but as she returned toward us, she struggled to hit the brake with her foot; the pole that ran from the hand control to the brake was getting in her way. In a panic, she reached for the hand control for the brake but grabbed the gas instead. The car flew forward and Mandy was losing control of it. And she was headed straight toward the three of us on the grass!

I was frozen. If I could have run, I would have. But unable to, I just sat there and screamed.

"Mandy, stop the car! Stop the car!"

Christie jumped up and tried to yank me and the chair out of the way, but we had put the brakes on the chair and couldn't get the wheels unlocked fast enough. There was nothing any of us could do except continue screaming at Mandy to stop the car.

She couldn't do it.

Bam!

The car struck me and the chair hard enough and low enough that I was launched into the air. When I came down I landed hard on the hood, rolled up it a couple times, then rolled down it before tumbling to the ground, a few feet in front of one of the tires…which were still moving! As I lay there, assuming that I was going to be run over, Mandy somehow managed to find the brake. I don't know if she found the hand control or the actual floor brake, but she brought the car to a complete stop about two inches from my body.

Mandy put it in park and jumped out of the car screaming hysterically.

"Missy! Missy! Are you okay?"

"Yeah, I think so," I said as I lay on the ground. I looked at my hand. "But you broke my fingernail!"

Everyone looked at each other as if waiting for someone to give permission to laugh…and then we all did.

The incident could have ended up being a tragic one, but with nobody seriously hurt, we were able to laugh about it and move on. Except we didn't laugh enough to keep the tape of it. I had mentioned that the guy who was with us recorded me driving. Well, he recorded Mandy's escapades, too. As much as I wish we had that tape today to laugh at, we erased it as soon as we returned to our cabin. We weren't sure that the camp leaders would have seen much humor in it.

*****

Another memorable and stressful moment that was averted with laughter happened one day when I was pregnant with our first child, Logan. Josh and I were both home because I was supposed to go to the hospital later that afternoon to have my labor induced. But, that morning, my face had turned red and I felt chills. Those were a couple of telltale signs that something unusual was happening with my body. I had a pretty good idea (and I was correct) what was going on.

"Josh," I calmly called to him from the bedroom. "I think I'm going into labor."

Uh-oh.

With Logan being our first child, Josh didn't fully understand what it meant when a woman was going into labor. Yes, it means you need to get to the hospital because you're about to have a baby. But it probably does not mean the baby is going to pop out in the next six seconds.

"We have to go now! I'll get the bags! You get in your chair. I'll lock up the house. Meet me at the car!" He was spitting out orders in his southern drawl like the middle school football coach that he was. Fortunately, he was on my team. Unfortunately, this was his first game at the professional level.

"The car keys! Where are they!" he yelled from the kitchen.

"I don't know!" I yelled back to him.

"You had them last!"

"No, I didn't!" I shouted. "You did!"

"We can't go anywhere without the keys!" he cried, stating the obvious.

"What do you want me to do?" I replied.

"Tell me where the keys are!"

Seriously?

"Look where they always are!" I said.

About twenty seconds went by before I heard his voice again.

"Found them!" Like I figured, they were right where they always were—between the couch cushions in the living room. They always go from the car ignition to his pocket to between the couch cushions—every single time.

I wheeled myself through the house as he ran circles around me trying to get my stuff together. When I got outside he came running behind me, literally tossed his can of Coke into the car, lifted me into the passenger seat, and slammed the door shut before running back in to get the bags.

"Be right back!" I heard him yell on the other side of the window.

With silence for the first time in a few minutes, I sat back, closed my eyes, and took several deep breaths. *We'll make it there. Just relax*, I told myself. *Just relax.*

But then…

That noise. What was it? My eyes popped open. It was a hissing sound, like air being released from something. I searched around the car—and there it was, on the floor next to me. And on my pants! The Coke was shooting out of the can! Are you kidding me? It must have been shaken up while Josh was trying to gather everything, and when he tossed it into the car, it punctured. With Coke spraying all over me, I grabbed the can, opened my door, and flung it onto the lawn just as Josh was charging out of the house with the bags. He witnessed my horrific atrocity.

"Missy!" he cried angrily. "What did you just do?"

"I threw out your stupid Coke!"

"What for?"

"Because it was spewing everywhere! It's all over the car! It's all over me! Look at it!" I said, pointing to it on the grass. "It's still coming out!"

You have to understand that next to our children and me, Josh loves nothing more than Coke. And on days the boys push him to the brink of insanity, Coke probably ranks higher. In fact, on days I push him too far…

Anyway, appearing dissatisfied with my response—I guess hanging on to an exploding can of Coke is better than no Coke at all in Josh's eyes—and despite our car and me being soaked in high fructose corn syrup and the can now serving as a sprinkler for our lawn, Josh calmly set down the bags, turned around, and walked methodically into the house. After a very long minute or so, he emerged from the front door…yes, with another can of Coke. He gently set the Coke down on the ground, calmly walked the bags to the back of the car, neatly loaded them and the wheelchair in, returned to pick up his Coke, and got into the car.

"Are…you…kidding…me?" I said slowly in a soft voice, but with a glare that could have sliced through his new can. He looked at me with his puppy dog eyes. "What? What did I do?" That's when I burst into uncontrollable laughter. After all of the tension, mayhem, yelling, and mess in the car and on my clothes—and let's not forget that a baby was on the way—it was getting a new can of Coke that had calmed him down and had made me laugh so hard that I thought I might give birth in the car.

*****

Look at the four stories I just shared. If all I had told you was that we laughed in our support group at school, we laughed after getting into a car accident, we laughed after Mandy plowed into me with a car, and we laughed on the way to the hospital as I was in labor, you would probably think we were insane or, at the very least, insensitive toward the situations we were in. But, after giving you the story behind each one, you can see how the laughter was not only okay, but it helped eliminate some tense moments.

Think about what would have happened if we had gone the other direction with our attitudes. How helpful would that support group have been if we all had come in each day and done nothing but complain and cry and talk about how unfair life was? Don't get me wrong—we did some of that, and we deserved to do some of that, but mixing in humor helped us find joy and purpose in our own lives and in each other.

What if, after the car accident, Taylor had jumped out of the car and verbally or physically assaulted the woman who hit us? Even if Taylor had still made the "she's paralyzed" comment, I doubt they would have been laughing about it since Taylor's negative attitude would have already set the tone for their interaction. The incident involving Mandy hitting me with the car had the potential to cause a lot of problems between all of us (Mandy and me, Christie and

Mandy, the car owner and all of us) if we hadn't seen the humor in what had happened. And how healthy would it have been for our baby and me if Josh and I had gotten into a big fight all the way to the hospital about something as silly as a Coke can?

I think an ideal question to ask yourself in every negative, high-anxiety situation is: "Can I laugh about this and move on?" The answer isn't always going to be yes. Many times it will be no, especially so soon after it happens. But by repeatedly asking yourself that question as you navigate the issue over time, you keep the door open to releasing that negative energy much sooner. Time can heal wounds if you are willing to let it. Don't be afraid to laugh at something, even if you once couldn't have imagined being able to do so.

*****

Author Kurt Vonnegut Jr. once said: "Laughter and tears are both responses to frustration and exhaustion...I myself prefer to laugh, since there is less cleaning up to do afterward."

When Logan was old enough to walk and I was home alone with him, he caused me a tremendous amount of frustration and exhaustion every day. He got into everything, as all toddlers do, but it's much more difficult to corral him when he can move quickly and I can't jump from my chair to chase him down. While there were some days I cried because of my limitations, I realized that I had to make a choice for my own health: continue crying, which was doing nothing but wearing me out mentally and physically, or laugh at some of the things he did—and maybe even join in the humor.

One of his favorite things to do after he did something he shouldn't have done was run away from me as fast as he could and plop himself on the floor behind the chair in the corner of the living room. Why there? Because he was smart enough to know that Mama's wheelchair couldn't fit back there. I could get close, but not close enough to reach him. This was pretty much a daily occurrence, and it frustrated me to no end. An able-bodied mom could just go behind the chair and grab her son and put him in his room, but I was involved in a game of tag that I was losing every day. *This is ridiculous*, I thought to myself. *There has to be another way to handle this.* That's when I came up with an idea.

One day, when Logan talked back to me, I wheeled myself toward him. As he took off toward the chair, I went back in the kitchen and grabbed a long-handled fly swatter I had just bought. I returned to the living room and positioned myself as close to him as I could. As he smirked at me, thinking he'd gotten away with his bad behavior again, I pulled out the fly swatter and began swatting. Not trying to squish him like a bug, of course, but just trying to get him out from behind the chair. It worked.

"Hey! Stop it! That's not fair!" he cried. He ran from behind the chair and into his bedroom, where I made him stay until he apologized for talking back. The image of me swatting at my son with a fly swatter to get him out from behind a chair is one that still makes me laugh, and I had to do everything in my power not to laugh as I was doing it. Had I continued to yell and chase him and let him get away with things because I couldn't reach him, I would have felt like an inadequate mother who had no authority over her own son. Changing my mindset to Vonnegut's "I myself prefer to laugh" made all the difference.

Laughter isn't always appropriate, but it can often be worked into many situations at the right time. Even most funerals today are referred to by ministers and families as a "celebration of life" rather than a somber final good-bye. It's a way to try to put smiles on people's faces, to laugh at the good times, and to bring some happiness to an otherwise very sad time. Don't wait for a funeral to laugh at or to let go of things. Celebrate life now, and laugh a lot while doing it.

Take Action!
Laugh

ℒ

Activity #1: You may have heard the saying, "Laughter is the best medicine." With a small group, research the physiological benefits of laughter. Use that research to create a script for a sixty-second infomercial on the benefits of laughter. You can simply read the script to the class or have someone read it while others act it out.

Activity #2: Discuss as a class the difference between laughing *with* someone and laughing *at* someone. What are the emotions that go with each? After the discussion, write on a piece of paper something funny that happened to you that you don't mind sharing—something that you were able to laugh at yourself. Turn the papers in to your teacher and have him or her read each one. After hearing each one, try to guess who wrote it. Once somebody guesses yours correctly, share with the class how you felt when the incident occurred and how you were able to laugh at yourself.

Journal Entry: Identify your top three stressors. They could include a sibling who annoys you, a close friend who is slow to respond to texts, a classmate who is always bugging you about something during class, a neighbor who cuts his grass at 7 A.M. on a Saturday. How would your day improve if you chose to change your response from anger, frustration, tears, etc., to laughter?

Be Optimistic

"Optimism is the faith that leads to achievement. Nothing can be done without hope and confidence."
– Helen Keller

S A PARAPLEGIC, I can do just about anything, including anything any able-bodied person can do. I just may have to do it a little differently, and it may take me a little longer. I have climbed a tree, ridden a horse, water-skied, driven a car, mowed the lawn, taken karate lessons, swam in a pool, played basketball, ridden on a roller coaster, harvested crops on a farm, played flute in a marching band, danced till I couldn't dance anymore, and jumped out of an airplane. Okay, I didn't really jump out of an airplane, but I could if I weren't afraid to freefall from five thousand feet in the air. And I really did do all of that other stuff. Seriously, challenge me to do something and I will usually at least give it a try. If, as you read that list, you asked yourself, "How did she do *that*?" I can tell you that it started with an optimistic attitude.

Admittedly, in the early weeks and months of my paralysis, a lot of doubt and frustration consumed me. In many ways, I had to learn how to live all over again. From the simple things, like entering and exiting buildings, to the more complex, like going to the bathroom, nothing would ever be the same as it once was. I mentioned that I even had an emotional breakdown in the hospital a couple weeks after the shooting, bawling my eyes out about everything that had happened—the shooting, the screams in the lobby, the deaths of three people, and my paralysis. But my choices for the long run were to feel sorry for myself and seclude myself inside my home where I would accomplish nothing and likely amount to nothing, or to work hard at creating a new "normal" so that I could enjoy my life and become a significant contributor to society. Finding the optimism to do the latter wasn't—and still isn't—always easy, but it is always possible.

For some people, optimism comes naturally. They wake up each morning with a smile, look forward to their day, see nothing but the good in every person and situation they face, and drift to sleep at night with full hearts and happy dreams about tomorrow. Good for them, but kind of annoying, right? Especially when some of us have to really work hard at all of that.

If you wake me up before 8 A.M. on my day off, you may not like what you get. If you catch me right after work when I just finished counseling a student whose home life is in shambles and she is all I can think about, I might not be in the best frame of mind. But the good news is that optimism is an intangible element that is always there. No matter where you are, who you are with, or what mood you are in, optimism is free for your taking whenever you want.

There are a few specific ways that I find and fuel my optimistic attitude, which I will share through a few stories. The first is that I keep my life in perspective and am grateful for what I have. The second is that I never quit and always keep trying. The third is that I don't try to just avoid negativity, but instead I try to harness it and turn it into something positive.

*****

I like to cook dinner for my family and, fortunately, they like what I cook, even though it takes me longer to make than it does for Josh. I have to wheel myself back and forth across the kitchen, get ingredients or utensils out of cupboards or drawers that may be difficult to reach, stir food on the stove that I cannot see because the pot is above my eye level. If I drop something on the floor, I have to figure out a fast and creative way to retrieve it before the dog snags it (which means I have maybe two seconds at most), or I need to call someone for help. It's a lot of little things that an able-bodied person may take for granted that can be difficult for me to deal with.

But I keep it all in perspective because I can empathize with what others in more difficult situations may have to face. There are people with diseases or disabilities who can't get out of bed each day to cook for themselves. There are elderly people who can't cook because they can't stand up for long periods of time or are more susceptible to burns or cuts. There are people with food allergies who can't touch a lot of foods without having a severe reaction. Even I get frustrated because it takes me more than an hour to make what a cookbook declares to be a "30-minute meal," I remain optimistic during the process because I know that my situation could be worse.

When I was at Cardinal Hill, there was an older gentleman on my floor who had a disease that paralyzed him from the waist up. Paralysis from the waist down is fairly common. From the waist up was something I had never heard of. His condition made me realize how lucky I was. From my perspective, being able to move and use my arms and hands was far more important than having the use of my legs because I could take care of myself more easily. I can't imagine trying to take care of my children or being able to work or being able to cook a meal without having the use of my upper body.

In most situations we are in, we can likely find someone who is facing difficulties greater than ours. That doesn't mean that we cannot or should not be upset or frustrated about our challenges. But if we can keep them in perspective and create a more optimistic attitude, we can likely get through them more easily.

In another example, I had every right to be angry that Michael shot and paralyzed me. I was fifteen years old with dreams that had vanished as soon as that bullet hit my spine. I couldn't play organized soccer anymore. My role in the marching band was to sit on the sidelines and play the flute without marching on the field because I couldn't physically march. I couldn't run around and play with my friends after school because my legs no longer worked. But then I would think about the families of Nicole, Kayce, and Jessica, and what they would give to have their daughters back, even in a wheelchair. I still had the right to be angry about all those things I couldn't do anymore, but putting them in perspective helped me deal with that anger.

Keeping your anger or frustrations in perspective is, like many other things, easier said than done. When you are angry, you often just want to be angry. You don't want someone telling you that things could be worse. So be angry. It's okay. Let your emotions flow when you need to. But once you have caught your breath and have calmed down, try to adjust your mindset. Recognize everything positive about yourself and around you. This way of thinking will hopefully become more natural the more you do it, which will create a happier you.

*****

I talk to my students a lot about how to be optimistic during failure. We all fail. We fail tests, we fail to make a team we try out for, we fail to win the big game, we fail to make a relationship work, we fail to complete a task the way our parents ask us to. If you say that you have never failed at anything, then you have just failed at telling the truth.

Michael Jordan, arguably the greatest basketball player ever, failed to make his high school varsity team as a sophomore because the coaches determined he wasn't good enough. Famous actors Jim Carrey, Steve Carell, and Kevin Hart all auditioned for *Saturday Night Live* and were told thanks, but no thanks. Walt Disney was fired from a newspaper job because he was told he lacked imagination. Everyone fails. How you handle that failure—with optimism or defeat—will determine your path going forward.

How do we find optimism and hope during failure? One way is to keep trying. And how do we find the fortitude and motivation to keep trying? Not by doing the same thing over and over again, but by making adjustments. We swallow our pride and seek help from others. We continue to educate ourselves or physically work harder and smarter until we reach our goals.

When I first started to learn how to use a wheelchair, the therapists made me do wheelies from my room to the cafeteria each day. If my front two wheels hit the floor, I had to go back to my room and start over. The purpose was to teach me how to maneuver in places that didn't have ramps. Each time my wheels hit the floor, I was angry—really angry. But I kept working at it, asked the therapists questions about what I was doing wrong, and tried different methods to keep those front wheels up. Today, if you see me somewhere, ask me to do a wheelie. I can even spin in circles on two wheels when I want to show off.

If you say you studied for a test and failed, then you need to study longer or differently the next time, maybe enlisting the help of a classmate or parent to quiz you or tutor you, or studying in your quiet room instead of in front of the television. If you failed to make a team, talk to the coach about what you need to work on in the offseason to have a better shot of making it, and then follow his course of action. If you can't seem to make a relationship work with a boy or girl, a friend might be able to offer you some advice from a perspective you hadn't considered.

Notice that finding optimism requires some action on your part. Expecting things to change for the better without any effort isn't likely to happen. Seek out that person who can help. Ask that question that can make the difference.

Make that change that can send you in a new and better direction. You may have to take a risk and step out of your comfort zone, but once you do it, the reward can be significant. Sometimes you need to make a tweak; other times you need a major overhaul. Whatever you need, approach it from a fresh perspective and give it another shot. A simple change in mindset is oftentimes all that is necessary to succeed.

Of course, there are times when we are destined to not succeed in certain ventures, no matter what we do differently or how many times we try. If you didn't make the basketball team each of the last few years and you were the first one cut each time, the coach may say that you are simply not at the level of those on the team and likely never will be. If you accept his assessment, don't crawl into a hole and feel sorry for yourself. Instead, find something that you *are* good at.

Are you a failure if you stop trying out for the basketball team but join the bowling team? Of course not. In fact, congratulations for listening to the basketball coach and being optimistic about your chances of succeeding at something else. You've just added another chapter to your story. I had a friend who played baseball and basketball for a few years but just wasn't at the same level as his peers. Instead of getting discouraged, he switched to karate, which suited him perfectly. After several years of hard work and determination, he earned his black belt. He left his comfort zone and took a risk by switching sports and walking into a karate class where he knew nothing and nobody. But after a few classes he was in a new comfort zone, and it paid off big time.

If you have ever watched the popular and award-winning television show *The Middle*, Sue Heck epitomizes optimism. She is socially awkward. She is horrible at sports. She can't seem to fit in anywhere. Yet nothing derails her positive attitude. No matter how wrong things go for her, she always thinks her big break is right around the corner. Watch a few episodes of the show if you have never seen it and you will see what I mean. Though a fictional character, I know there are a lot of Sue Hecks in the world. I even see some of her in me. Keep your head up and keep trying. Block out the negatives and embrace the positives. Repeatedly tell yourself that you can do whatever it is that you want to accomplish.

*****

Turning something negative into something positive can be an enormous challenge. You are essentially not only trying to stop the momentum of a force, but reverse it. However, it can certainly be done.

Lately, I have been doing something unique with my students to help them turn their pessimism into optimism: we have been "flushing away" the negativity—figuratively and literally. For example, I had one boy who did not get along with his stepdad. They would argue a lot, and the boy would let every little thing his stepdad did annoy him. We discussed exactly what his stepdad did that got under his skin and the reaction the boy would normally have toward those things. We wrote each of them down on a piece of paper and talked about how the boy could only control his own reactions, not his stepdad's actions. Then we went into the bathroom and flushed the list down the toilet.

It may sound kind of silly, but it has been effective. It helped the boy see that he could escape that cycle of negativity he was entangled in if he so chose. Now, each time the stepdad does one of those annoying things, the boy smiles, pictures what we did, and says, "Nope. I already flushed that away. It's not going to bother me," and he moves on. While flushing words down a toilet really doesn't eliminate something, that action can change your viewpoint toward the negativity, which can create optimism. (If you don't like the idea of flushing a piece of paper down the toilet, another option is to hold a "funeral." Take the paper out back, say a few final words about how everything written on it is dead to you, and bury it.)

Something else you can do is bluntly ask yourself, "How can I turn this situation around into something positive?" On the surface, it may not seem possible, but when you put some effort and creativity into it and brainstorm with the idea that you *can* reverse the negative course of something, you will be pleasantly surprised at what you can accomplish.

For example, there was a beautiful memorial constructed in the courtyard at Heath High School after the shooting to keep the memories of the shooting victims alive. However, as the years went on, it was difficult for the school and district to fund the maintenance of it, causing it to deteriorate. Also, since it was in the middle of the school, nobody outside of the school could see it without an appointment. These issues upset a lot of people, and many were quick to point blame.

Nicole's sister, who didn't like what the memorial had become, decided that rather than complaining about it, she was going to try to do something about it. She went to the school board and expressed her concerns, along with some possible solutions. The board agreed to provide land and lighting across the street from the school for a new memorial that would be open to the public every day around the clock. They also agreed to let the families of the victims design the memorial. As a result of her effort, money was raised and several businesses donated time and materials to make it happen. Because Nicole's sister and her family let their optimism shine over any pessimism they may have had, they accomplished something that was a win for the families, the school district, and the entire community.

Here is one way to view turning a negative into a positive: have you ever seen a dead tree get put through a wood chipper? The tree's branches and trunk are cut into small pieces and tossed into the chipper, which turns them into mulch that can be used in flower beds. I view the dead tree as the negative; it no longer has any use as a dead tree. But once it's all chopped up, it turns into mulch—the positive—and it is instantly alive again with a new purpose.

Run any negativity you have through that chipper and turn it into something positive.

*****

I know that trying to be optimistic all the time, or at least more than you are now, can be mentally and even physically draining. We all may not be good at putting things in perspective, or at never giving up on something, or at turning a negative into a positive. So is it possible to be more optimistic simply by trying to avoid all that is negative? Absolutely, especially on social media.

One phrase I often see on social media is, "I'm so tired of all the negativity." And there has definitely been a lot of it lately. One solution is to simply ignore the garbage people thrust in front of you. If you are on Facebook or Instagram and see one negative post or photo after another, just keep scrolling. I do think it is important to know what is happening in the world, so don't completely block out important events just because they make you sad or angry. But take control of when you see those things.

For example, an actress or an athlete or a politician may do or say something that the media thinks is controversial. So then every person on social media feels the need to add his or her two cents with posts and comments and memes. These people will clog up your newsfeed all day long and get so ridiculous with their comments that it is difficult to even know what the truth is anymore. What I would suggest you do in that case is go to an independent news source that you know you can rely on and read the real story for yourself. Make your own judgment on it and ignore the insults people on social media are hurling toward one another. If you do your own research to find the truth and then go back to social media, it makes a lot of those posts and memes funny instead of annoying—because you have educated yourself and you know what is real.

Something else you can do to combat the negativity on social media is promote what makes you happy and optimistic just as strongly as those who are spewing negativity. I know people who each day post inspirational sayings, funny videos, cute pictures of their family, or jokes. When you scroll through your feed and find the string of pessimism broken by a video of cuddly kittens snuggling with puppies, it can remind you of all that is good and fuel your optimism, not to mention the optimism of your friends and followers.

Another logical option would be to just leave social media for an extended period of time. We are all so plugged in to absolutely everything that we are afraid we're going to miss something if we leave for any period of time. Trust me, as someone who lived in the age before the Internet and social media were even things, you won't be missing much if you turn off social media sites for a day or two. If that feels like it would be too long, try it for a few hours. Then, when you reconnect, check to see what you missed. You will likely see that you didn't miss anything pertinent. So then try it for a few more hours. Keep extending the time you are disconnected, and keep yourself busy during that time with some worthwhile projects. Eventually, it will become habit to look online a lot less, which will disrupt the constant flow of negativity.

*****

Being optimistic, especially in negative situations or around persistently negative people, can take a lot of time, effort, help from others, a shift in mindset—or all of them at once. Just know that no matter how down you or those around you are, the choice for you to be optimistic is always there. Being negative doesn't mean good things can't happen to you, and being optimistic doesn't mean you are free from bad things happening, but I do find that you often reap what you sow. Negative attitudes will often result in negative consequences, and optimistic attitudes will usually bring a lot of good things your way.

Be as positive as you can however you can do it, and in every situation that you can. Before you know it, you will become one of those people for whom optimism comes naturally. I'm almost there…if I can just learn to love early mornings on my days off a little more.

Take Action!
Be Optimistic

ℰℒ

Activity #1: There were examples in this chapter of choices that I and others made to shift our thinking and attitudes from angry and negative to a more positive and empowered view. Write down five life lessons you learned in this chapter about optimism that you can refer to in the future when you are upset or frustrated about something.

Activity #2: We all know that listening to music can improve our moods and provide us with new and positive perspectives on whatever life throws at us. Create a playlist of ten of your favorite songs that encourage optimism. Which of the ten is your absolute favorite, and why?

Activity #3: Optimism is about taking control of your life. I had no control over the shooting, but I did have control over how I reacted to it—with pessimism or with optimism. Make a list of five obstacles or challenges you are facing today or have faced in the recent past. After you have identified the challenges, list ways in which you could turn those challenges into opportunities that could benefit you or others in the short or long term.

Journal Entry: Identify a situation toward which you seem to have a consistently negative attitude. How can you use some of the insights from this chapter to improve your outlook? Provide information about your situation and specific ideas you can implement to begin replacing those negative thoughts.

Be Kind

"You cannot do a kindness too soon, for you never know how soon it will be too late."
– Ralph Waldo Emerson

L IKE MANY CHRISTIAN CHURCHES, my church holds a service each Wednesday evening that I try to attend with my boys and Mandy's daughter, who is about Logan's age. Mandy or Josh will usually go with me, but on one particular Wednesday that they couldn't go, I took the kids myself. There is a separate worship service for the children, led by two women named Kristen and Alyssa, and I am an assistant to them.

On the way to the service, the kids were in rare form, even for as wild as they have been known to be. I don't know if they sneaked some extra candy into their bloodstreams before we left or if they just had a slow day at school that left them with a lot of pent up energy, but they were out of control—screaming, laughing, arguing, name-calling, poking, slapping. You name it, they were doing it. I gave them multiple warnings in the car and assumed that when we got into church, where they knew what kind of behavior was expected of them, they would straighten up.

They didn't. Not even close.

They were a major distraction during the entire youth service. I was so embarrassed that I apologized to Kristen and Alyssa multiple times. On the way home, I yelled at the kids like I had never yelled before. I was angry with them and with myself because I felt like a failure—not just as a youth leader, but as a mother. I hadn't been able to control my own kids, and in church of all places. They had brought out the worst in themselves, which brought out the worst in me, and I certainly wasn't proud of any of it.

Once I had calmed down and we got home, I had a lengthy talk with them about listening and empathy ("I was trying to teach other kids during the service; how do you think it made me feel to instead have to spend all night trying to get you all to behave? And how do you think it made them feel for me to have to continually stop teaching them in order to try to control you?"). I felt a responsibility to use what had happened as a teaching moment, but it also was an evening I wanted to forget.

The next day at work, still upset by what had happened, my boss came to my office.

"Missy, a couple of women just dropped this off for you," he said.

It was a vase of flowers. I was stunned. It wasn't my birthday or any other special occasion that I knew of. There was no card.

"Do you know who they are from?" I asked.

"It was two women who said they were from your church. They said they want you to know that they love you and that they hope your day is a better one today."

Kristen and Alyssa.

I was emotionally overwhelmed. I cried at their incredible thoughtfulness, then texted them to thank them.

"We just wanted to be there for you," Alyssa replied.

I reflected on the choices they could have made in reaction to what had happened at the service. They could have asked that my kids not come back, or that I bring someone with me next time to help me with them. They could have kindly said that they can handle the group on their own and that I don't have to worry about helping them, a polite way of telling me to take care of my own kids. They could have complained to each other behind my back and questioned my parenting skills. They could have posted something on social media about what a crazy night they had had at church, with me knowing full well what they were talking about.

But they aren't like that, and they never have been.

What they did instead was empathize with me. Then they used that empathy to show me a random act of kindness. Their one simple gesture of bringing me flowers instantly and completely changed my world.

Opening your heart to others through acts of kindness is one of the easiest things to do, especially when you follow the other principles. Being kind is so much simpler when you listen, when you are empathetic, when you can forgive, when you can laugh, and when you are optimistic. But being kind is also one principle that can stand alone more than the others because I believe we are all born inherently kind.

Even many of my day treatment students who are raised in difficult environments—where the violence and anger that surrounds them hardens their hearts—show their peers and me some act of kindness nearly every day. Their kind word, gesture, or smile may be infrequently scattered among the things they shouldn't say or do, but it's there.

Being kind to others is easy because it can be done at any time on any day for any reason. You could put this book down right now and text a kind message to a friend or family member. You could go outside and bring your neighbor's garbage cans from the curb to their house. You could go to the fridge to get yourself a snack and ask your brother if he would like you to get him anything. You could fold the pile of laundry your mom just washed and dried. You could pet a dog, pick up litter, wave to a random person, play a game with your kid sister, do the dishes, donate a book to a library, buy a candy bar for a friend. Heck, you could even just click "like" on a post someone made on social media that isn't getting many likes from others. As silly as that might sound on the surface in relation to kindness, you know how good it feels when people recognize what you have to say on social media.

I was on Facebook one day when I saw someone post, "Please comment on how we met." After commenting, I decided to post that statement to my wall to see what responses I would get. Within a day, I had one hundred fifty comments, and every single one warmed my heart. But it was the ones from my former day treatment students that got me choked up.

"Not something I'm very proud of, but day treatment," one guy said in response to how we had met. "I'm actually married now. I have two beautiful little girls, and I can say I actually like what I do for a living."

"When you first started at the day treatment center," another guy stated. "You were definitely my favorite person there and I am so glad to have met someone so kindhearted and genuinely caring."

"Way back in middle school. You came to talk to my school about your story and then you helped me through day treatment," a third guy said. "Helped me when I was on the streets. Thanks for all your help." He went on to say that he was living in Florida, he had just gotten engaged, and he wanted me to attend his wedding.

It took those who responded to my post maybe twenty to thirty seconds each to do so…and here I am months later still talking about what they had said because of the profound effect their words had on me.

*****

In the summer of 2015, Josh and I traveled to Little Rock, Arkansas, for a speaking engagement I had at a high school. It was during our ninth wedding anniversary, so we decided to make a little trip of it without the boys. After checking into our hotel, we boarded a hotel van that was going to take us to a nearby restaurant for dinner. There was another person staying at the hotel who boarded the bus with us to go to the same restaurant. He was an older guy on a business trip. We said hi to him, he said hi back, and then a conversation started. He asked us who we were and why we were in town. We told him this was going to be our anniversary dinner. He told us that he was divorced. He said he was on the road so much because of his job that he and his wife just couldn't make their marriage work. Though it had been a few years since they had separated, he still seemed sad about it, but he was genuinely happy that we were celebrating nine years together.

When we got to the restaurant, he met up with his party and we said our good-byes. After Josh and I had a lovely dinner, we asked our waiter for the check.

"Oh, there's no check," the waiter cheerfully said. "It has been paid for."

When we asked by whom, he said a gentleman who had just left. When he described him to us, we knew it had been the man we had met in the van. He didn't tell us he was going to do it. He didn't stick around long enough for us to thank him. He didn't tell the waiter to tell us who had done it. We looked for him when we went back to the hotel, but we never saw him again.

I think his kind gesture was triggered by our story and how it related to his life. His marriage didn't work, but ours did, and he appreciated that. He saw a couple who had made it this far and he wanted to celebrate with us. He saw us about to have a nice evening, and he wanted to make it even nicer. I can't tell you what an awesome feeling it was to know that a stranger had done that for us. It's an act of kindness that I will never forget, and an idea I will use to do the same for another couple one day.

*****

As you can imagine, so much kindness was directed toward me and my family after the shooting. There were the cards and gifts. A local car dealership gave our family a van that was handicap accessible. Strangers and friends alike built an addition onto our home to make it handicap accessible so that we wouldn't have to move. There were kids who carried my books to class, who carried my lunch tray, who held doors open for me, who pushed my chair up ramps. There were those who sent me flowers, cooked meals for my family, and donated money to help with medical bills. There were doctors and nurses who cared for me, and physical therapists who patiently worked with me to get better. There were teachers who taught me around my doctor and therapy appointments. Our principal even gave me keys to my own bathroom when I returned to school because he knew that would be a difficult issue for me that would require some privacy. And my siblings and parents—oh my goodness! Their lives revolved around me and my needs every single day!

Two of the most inspiring acts of kindness done for me personally were from my sisters, Christie and Mandy. Already in college and well on her career path, Christie abruptly quit school to help my parents take care of me. It wasn't something my parents or I asked her to do or even considered asking her to do. She simply saw the need that our family had and did what she felt she needed to do for us. It was one of the most selfless acts I have ever witnessed.

Mandy helped Christie take care of me at home, but she also made sure that nothing changed for me socially. Mandy was not just my twin sister, but my best friend, and that didn't change after the shooting. She didn't leave me behind to go out with friends. She didn't let me sit home and feel sorry for myself. She faced situations head on with me. She helped me to still be a teenager and to not be defined by my disability. She never once said, "We aren't going to do this because you are in a wheelchair." She said, "We are going to find a way to do this together." She gave me the motivation I needed every single day to live my life, and she still treats me that way today.

*****

Here are a few more examples of kindness:

One time I helped a group in Paducah get a handicap-accessible playground by attending a city council meeting and sharing my story as a disabled mother who often struggles to move with her children on a playground. I cannot quantify how much my presence at the meeting helped—several other people did nearly all of the work—but I certainly think that having a mother from Paducah in a wheelchair there aided their cause. It took a few hours out of my life to drive up to Paducah and attend the meeting, but it provided something for my hometown community that was needed and could last generations. It still makes me feel good today to know that I contributed, even if just in a small way, toward making the playground come to fruition simply by giving some of my time.

Another example would be when my grandpa died. Mandy and I were in sixth grade. His death was difficult for all of us, especially for our grandma. They had been married for decades and she relied on him for everything, most notably his companionship. We knew that without him, she would be very lonely. To help her transition into a life without him, Mandy and I started going to her house on Friday nights. We'd watch TV, do crossword puzzles, bake sweet treats...anything to keep her entertained and busy. We would then spend the night and make pancakes Saturday morning before heading home. This became a weekly tradition. Sure, there were other things that a couple of teenage girls might have rather been doing on their Friday nights, but we thoroughly enjoyed our time with our grandma because it made her happy, which in turn made us happy. It wasn't a big sacrifice on our part because we loved spending time with our grandma. But that time we spent with her meant even more to her. It filled a huge void in her life and helped relieve some of her sadness.

Something I do on a regular basis that costs me nothing but time is read my social media messages each week and respond to kids who are seeking advice on how to handle a school bully. It's not something I get paid for, and giving them advice is not always easy to do because I don't know the whole story behind what they are telling me, but I do the best that I can to help them. It would be easy to say to myself, *I get too many requests for this kind of thing and I simply cannot help everybody*, but my heart won't let me do that. What will happen if I ignore them? They often come to me because they don't know where else to turn. If my time is limited or if I don't feel like my advice is helping, I will at the very least try to tell them who they should talk to (a principal, teacher, friend) so they can seek help closer to home.

I consider the talks I give at schools, churches, and businesses to be acts of kindness. While I generally do get paid for them since they are partly how I make my living, I keep my cost as low as I can so that anyone can afford to hear me speak. I've been told by many in the speaking business that I don't charge enough, but the impact I am making is far more important to me. When I receive messages from students after a talk that I changed their lives, or even saved their lives, it reminds me that I am making a difference and that I need to keep doing what I am doing.

*****

I will never be able to directly repay all of the people who have helped me, but that's another cool thing about kindness—those dishing it out don't, or shouldn't, expect anything in return. Someone once said, "When you do something out of love, you don't count the cost." If you can reciprocate someone's kindness in some way when they need you, by all means, do it! If you cannot, then pay it forward to someone who could benefit from your kind heart. That's how kindness spreads. That's how love spreads.

There is a gentleman named Bob Votruba who started a nonprofit organization after the 2007 shooting at Virginia Tech called One Million Acts of Kindness. In a nutshell, Bob quit his job to travel the country in an old school bus promoting kindness in schools, businesses, and public venues. His goal is for each person in the world to perform one million acts of kindness in their lifetime. Let's say you are fifteen years old now and expect to live to be eighty. That gives you sixty-five years to perform one million acts, or roughly forty-two acts of kindness per day. Sound unreasonable?

It's really not.

Think about your day tomorrow and where you will be. What acts of kindness can you perform? Before you even leave the house for school, you can smile at your parents and say good morning instead of grumbling at or ignoring them. You can let your sibling use the bathroom first. You can do quick chores that your parents may normally do, like put the dishes that are in the sink into the dishwasher or feed the dog or straighten the living room or take the trash to the curb. Maybe you can carry something to the car for your mom or open her door for her. Instead of turning the radio to your favorite station, you can turn it to hers. You can engage her in conversation on the way to school. You can thank her for the ride. Once in school, there are all sorts of kind gestures you can do. You can say hello to people, hold doors open, help someone carry their belongings into the building, pick up and throw away a piece of garbage, compliment someone on how they look, let someone ahead of you in the breakfast line, sit with someone in the cafeteria who is sitting alone, or congratulate someone on an academic or athletic accomplishment. I've just given you nearly twenty ideas and your day has barely started.

Forty-two acts may seem like a lot in the beginning because you may have to make a conscious effort to hit that number, but over time it will become habit. You not only will surpass forty-two acts most days, but you will enjoy doing every one of them as you make people happy. And the best part is that your kindness toward others will often spread like wildfire.

If you need more inspiration on acts of kindness you can do for others, just use the Internet to look up "acts of kindness" or "random acts of kindness," and you will find plenty of simple and creative ideas.

*****

Doing acts of kindness, especially ones so big that they can be labeled as "service projects," can be fun and fulfilling because you are putting yourself to work for others who need you. But it's getting started that often intimidates people because they are too shy ("I want to do it, but I'm nervous about it..."), they worry that they might mess up something ("I've never worked in a soup kitchen before..."), or they are afraid they won't do as good of a job as needed ("How am I supposed to help build a Habitat for Humanity home when I can't even keep my own room clean?"). So here are a few tips to help you begin:

- Find a project you think you might like to do, and then find someone you know who has done it who can give you the confidence you need to get started. For example, if you want to build a home with Habitat for Humanity, put a message on social media or email friends and family that you would like to try it, but that you would first like to learn more about it from someone who has done it. You will be shocked to find how many people have done it or know someone who has and are willing to help you get involved. You may even find that someone you know is about to do it again soon and is willing to let you tag along.
- Tell friends or family what you would like to do and recruit them to do it with you. Tackling a fear is much easier when you have others to tackle it with.

- Nonprofit organizations are always in need of volunteers, and they often advertise for help on their websites or in the media. There are also websites that are dedicated to matching people with volunteer opportunities.
- Look to volunteer for an organization that might be related to the career you are considering. It will give you some extra motivation to reach out to someone who can help you volunteer, and it will enable you to do something that is more in your comfort zone. For example, if you want to go into nursing, contact your local hospital to see what opportunities they might have available. Hospitals are always looking for volunteers. That doesn't mean you are going to be allowed to perform the duties of nurses, but just getting your foot in the door and being around nurses could help you down the road. Or, as another example, if you think you want to be a veterinarian, consider volunteering at your local animal shelter. Volunteering at a young age in a field you think you want to pursue cannot only help those you are trying to help, but it can also help you decide if that is what you really want to do with your life. You may find that working in an animal shelter is too emotional for you to handle, so being a vet may not be the best course for you to take.

Think about what service you can do for others on any given day. Do you have an elderly neighbor whose flower garden needs to be weeded? Neighbors who work all day and whose dog you can walk while they are gone? Litter that can be picked up throughout the neighborhood? Someone who is sick, even with just a cold, who could use a hot meal that you could make on your own or with a parent? A teacher at school whose classroom could use cleaning at the end of the day a couple times a week? A friend who is struggling in a class and could use some tutoring? These are all ideas close to home or school that wouldn't take a whole lot of effort. And imagine the possibilities when you think even bigger! I don't know too many people or organizations that won't accept free help. And I don't know too many people who don't get a tremendous amount of satisfaction by giving free help to those who need it.

One more idea I want to give you: don't ever underestimate the power and value of your own story, and use it to be kind to others. I know my story is a very public one that has received a lot of media attention and is very unique. Your story may not have the "public" or "media" aspects attached to it, but it is certainly unique. What in your story could you share with someone to help them conquer a difficult situation? If you were bullied once and you see another person being bullied, you may be surprised at how simply sharing your experience could help them. If you were ever the victim of anything and you know someone going through the exact same thing, they may love to hear from you so that they know they are not alone. Telling your story can also be very healing for you and can help you make some sense out of difficult or even tragic events you have endured.

Remember that your story is different from everyone else's, which means you have something unique to offer. Don't ever think your story is not good enough, interesting enough, popular enough, or filled with enough lessons to make a difference in someone else's life. There are people who can learn from you. Use your story for kindness.

*****

A final thought: as you open your heart to the people around you with your kind words and gestures, enjoy every moment of it. The primary purpose of an act of kindness is to better the life of the person you are doing it for, but there is nothing wrong with you feeling a sense of pleasure and pride in what you have done. Don't brag to others about it. Don't tell yourself what a great person you are. Don't look for publicity. You should even consider doing it anonymously if you can—there can be a tremendous amount of satisfaction doing something for somebody without them knowing it was you who did it. However you do it, know that it's okay to enjoy the experience of watching someone benefit from your kindness. It will make you feel good inside, and it will likely encourage you to want to do it again or to even strive to do something bigger and better next time.

A friend of mine, author Ron Franscell, once said, "Whatever inspires us to do good instead of evil is a worthwhile inspiration." If the self-satisfaction of seeing others benefit from your kindness is what inspires you, keep doing what you are doing.

Take Action!
Be Kind

༄

Activity #1: As important as it is to be kind to others, it is also helpful to be mindful of how others express kindness to us. Make a gratitude list of ten acts of kindness you have experienced during the past week and share the list with the class. These do not have to be anything monumental. Have you ever experienced a small act of kindness from a stranger that made your day? Maybe someone let you in front of them in line or picked up something for you that you dropped on the floor. The more we are aware of kindnesses we receive and express gratitude for them, the more aware we will become of how we can express kindness to others.

Activity #2: Create a "Kindness Diary" as a class. The diary will be a large space on a classroom wall. At the end of each day, write on a Post-it something kind you did for someone (if you did more than one act, use a separate Post-it for each). Have your teacher collect them and stick them to the wall. These acts can be any acts of kindness, large or small, that you did toward anybody inside or outside of school. However, try to be as creative as you can, writing down acts you did that could make your classmates say, "I am going to do that for someone one day."

Activity #3: Show clips (or all) of the 2000 film *Pay It Forward*. Discuss what the junior high school class in the film did, and discuss some ideas that you as a class may be able to do to "pay it forward."

Journal Entry: How did the acts of kindness that people did for you this week set the tone for you each day? How did the acts that you performed for others affect their mood, and how did being kind to them make you feel? What are some acts of kindness you would like to do for others this week?

Epilogue

"Don't be afraid of new ideas. Be afraid of old ideas. They keep you where you are and stop you from growing and moving forward. Concentrate on where you want to go, not on what you fear."
– Tony Robbins

NEW IDEAS CAN BE scary because they may not conform to what society says is right or trendy or "in." They can instill in us a fear that prevents us from letting them ever leave our minds, or that causes us to quit after one unsuccessful attempt. But new ideas, as Mr. Robbins says, are what make us grow and move forward.

I almost didn't write this book because of fear. Fear that I would say something that could be misinterpreted. Fear that I would say something that someone with a PhD in empathy or forgiveness would disagree with. Fear that I would forget to say something important that I meant to say. Fear that my words would have little impact on anybody.

But I overcame that fear when, months after the presidential election that ripped apart families and friendships, people of all walks of life still weren't getting along. In fact, they were nastier than ever toward one another. There was little listening or empathizing or forgiving. Laughs were few and far between. Optimism and kindness were absent. And those attitudes were trickling down to our youth. Something had to be done.

I concentrated on where I wanted to go, which was to try to bring love and peace into people's lives by sharing my personal stories and perspectives. I knew I didn't have all the answers. I don't have a high-level degree. I can't solve everyone's problems. But what I do have are unique and compelling experiences that for years have positively affected a lot of lives and could continue to do so.

Now that I have shared them with you, I need your help.

I need you to take anything good you have learned from me and spread it far and wide. Start within yourself. Find that listener, that empathizer, that kind person inside of you, and let that person shine. Lead by example. Don't let pessimists bring you down or tell you that you are wasting your time. Be persistent. Believe that this can work. People will follow your lead. It may start with just one person, one friend, one family member, but everything has to start somewhere.

Remember, people want this. They want love. They want peace. They will appreciate when you give it to them, and they will eventually realize they can give it just as easily. Some people will be tougher to crack than others, but stick with it. Don't give up. At worst, you will produce a more peaceful and loving and satisfying life for yourself. At best, your example will stretch around the globe.

If you are at home right now, look out your front window at someone walking by. If you are in a car, look at the person in the car next to you. If you are at school or in the library, pick out someone at a nearby desk or table whom you don't know. Wherever you are, realize that the people around you have their own stories, ones that are very different from yours and mine. Stories that you may never know but that influence who they are, what they believe, how they behave, and who they will become.

- Respect that about them.
- Listen to them if they need an ear.
- Empathize with them when they need some empathy.
- Forgive them when they wrong you.
- Laugh with them.
- Be optimistic around them.
- And be kind to them.

If it is not going to start with you, where is it going to start?

"Let peace begin with me, let this be the moment now. With every step I take, let this be my solemn vow: to take each moment and live each moment in peace eternally. Let there be peace on earth, and let it begin with me."

Take Action!
Your Legacy

Journal Entry: I discussed in the chapter on empathy how I often ask my students what they want their legacy to be. Keeping in mind everything that you have learned in this book, what do you want your legacy to be? How do you want people you encounter throughout your life to remember you? What are you doing today to contribute in a positive way to your legacy? What can you improve upon, and how will you do it?

Acknowledgments

"I am always comforted by realizing that there are still so many helpers—so many caring people in this world."
–Fred Rogers

Writing a book such as this is not a one-person job. There is no way I could have produced this without the help of so many. Thank you to:

Josh, Logan, and Carter. You three are my reason for living. Thank you for your patience throughout this project and for supporting me every step of the way.

My students in day treatment. Your contributions to this book are going to aid other students across the country and around the world. Be proud of yourselves for your effort in helping me make this a success.

William Croyle, who has helped me craft my words for more than a decade. I have said to you before that it's like you're inside my head—you are a master at knowing exactly what I want to say and at just the right time.

Tim Hanner, for your guidance and wisdom in my effort to make this a book that will resonate with all youth, and for pushing me to make each draft better than the previous one.

Debra Croyle, Carol Daria, and Meighan Ottiger, for your superior editing skills that made these pages shine.

Mark and Lorna Reid with AuthorPackages for the beautiful cover and interior design. Thank you for sharing your incredible talents.

Leslie Hughes, Michael Laughlin, Kim Mott, and Jessica Dykes, for all of your help creating and developing the lessons at the end of each chapter. You are some of the best educators around, and I am grateful that you were a part of this.

Alyssa Ianiro, Helen Lambron, Lois Qualben, Lillian Hale, Mya Hale, Valerie Keller, Catherine Keller, Sandra Rivera, Morgan Guess, Susan Guess, and Lisa Kovach. Your input in making this book the best it could be was invaluable.

The NaviGo Student Board of Directors in Northern Kentucky. You are some of our nation's brightest students, and it showed with the assistance you provided me in designing this book.

To the many people who endorsed the book: Tim Hanner, Heather Martin, C. Ed Massey, Bill Bond, Phil Blaylock, Bob Votruba, Susan Guess, and Ashley Cech. Your kind words warmed my heart. I am honored to know you and deeply thankful for your friendship.

To the many others who helped in various ways, large and small. Your contributions are greatly appreciated.

Printed in Great Britain
by Amazon

19794846R00092